"Here is a st                                          marriage
partner may                                          your marriage than everything you do after getting married."

—Neil Clark Warren, Ph.D.

# FINDING THE LOVE OF YOUR LIFE
## Ten Principles for Choosing the Right Marriage Partner

"... *And they lived happily ever after.*" It makes for a good fairy tale, but in reality, it takes a lot of hard work and commitment to beat the odds against staying married today. *FINDING THE LOVE OF YOUR LIFE* can help you determine whether you and your Mr. or Ms. Right are truly compatible when you explore *the seven most common causes of faulty mate selection*:

1. The decision to get married is made too quickly
2. The decision is made at too young an age
3. One or both persons are too eager to get married
4. One or both may be choosing a mate to please some-one else
5. The experience base is too narrow
6. The couple has unrealistic expectations
7. One or both may have unaddressed personality or behavior problems

*FINDING THE LOVE OF YOUR LIFE* helps you take the crucial first step to a successful marriage—finding a partner who's your ideal match—and puts you in control of the most important decision of your life!

# FINDING THE *Love* OF YOUR LIFE

## TEN PRINCIPLES FOR CHOOSING THE RIGHT MARRIAGE PARTNER

## NEIL CLARK WARREN, PH.D.

POCKET BOOKS

New York   London   Toronto   Sydney   Tokyo   Singapore

POCKET BOOKS, a division of Simon & Schuster Inc.
1230 Avenue of the Americas, New York, NY 10020

Copyright © 1992 by Neil Clark Warren

Published by arrangement with Focus on the Family Publishing

Warren, Neil Clark.
    Finding the love of your life / Neil Clark Warren.
      p.  cm.
    Includes bibliographical references.
    ISBN 0-671-89201-0
    1. Marriage—United States.   2. Mate selection—United States.
    3. Love.  I. Title.
HQ734.W3175   1994
646.7'7—dc20                    94-19506
                                          CIP

First Pocket Books trade paperback printing December 1994

10  9  8  7  6  5  4  3  2  1

POCKET and colophon are registered trademarks of Simon & Schuster Inc.

Printed in the U.S.A.

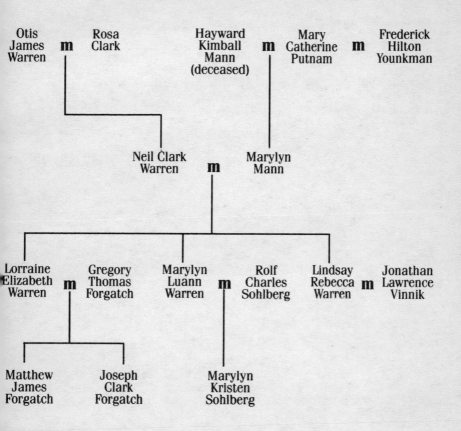

Otis James Warren **m** Rosa Clark

Hayward Kimball Mann (deceased) **m** Mary Catherine Putnam **m** Frederick Hilton Younkman

Neil Clark Warren **m** Marylyn Mann

Lorraine Elizabeth Warren **m** Gregory Thomas Forgatch

Marylyn Luann Warren **m** Rolf Charles Sohlberg

Lindsay Rebecca Warren **m** Jonathan Lawrence Vinnik

Matthew James Forgatch

Joseph Clark Forgatch

Marylyn Kristen Sohlberg

These are the primary people in my life, and they have taught me virtually everything I know about love. This book is dedicated to them.

# *Contents*

# Acknowledgments

My friends and family know that when I write a book, it is a community project. I read sections of hot-off-the-press chapters to them and invite their comments; they tell me relevant stories about themselves which I ask them to write up for inclusion. Now and then, when I'm feeling confident and safe, I ask them to read a chapter or two—and "give it to me straight."

More friends and family contributed to this book than I can say, but some of them are Lorrie Forgatch, Luann Warren-Sohlberg, Lindsay Warren-Vinnik, Dr. Loy McGinnis, Catherine Clement and Dr. Paul Clement, Dr. Jerry North, Russ Reid, Dr. Paul Roberts, Joyce Penner and Dr. Cliff Penner, Kristine Penner, Howard and Nell Privett, Carol Heit, Margery Proctor, Rick Thyne, Brendan Thyne, Kurt Johns, Pat Self and Dr. Lewis Smedes.

Hans Ritschard and Dr. Angela Rose tracked down scores of research articles. Their assistance was vital.

Keith Wall of Focus on the Family Publishing deserves special mention. He edited the manuscript and became a full partner in the project. Gwen Weising carefully coordinated each phase of publication.

My wife, Marylyn, not only read every word and made substantive contributions to every chapter, but never quit believing in the value of the effort.

Finally, I wish to thank my clients for sharing so deeply of themselves. Their stories are scrambled and coalesced so they will not recognize themselves, but it is their voices that are being heard.

# *Introduction*

Every person I know yearns for love! And the most obvious place to search for it is in marriage. In fact, more than 90 percent of all the people in the United States will marry at least once during their lifetime.

A recent *Los Angeles Times* poll sampled the opinions of more than 2,000 American adults. The overwhelmingly popular answer to the question about "their main goal in life" was "to be happily married." Marriage involves incredible potential for happiness, but there is also an enormous risk of failure. When two people fall in love and decide to spend the rest of their lives together, they can create unsurpassed joy for themselves and their children—or unspeakable havoc for everyone involved.

Listen to these true stories of love and marriage that turned out so differently:

### Jessica's Story

"I married a man who is utterly comfortable with who he is and delights in discovering who I am. I was attracted to John because his life has integrity, he's hard working and fun loving, and he loves me completely as I am. Early in our marriage my father said, 'I've never seen you so happy.' My brother commented, 'This is the buoyant sister I remember.' The explanation is simple: For the first time in my life I feel unconditionally and unreservedly loved. John and I are more alike than not, but the differences make life more interesting than threatening. Our commitment is explicitly to each other first, believing that a solid relationship enables us to cope with the inevitable challenges from demanding family and work situations."

*Barbara's Story*

"Gary was impeccably dressed and groomed, self-assured and confident, traveled and sophisticated. He appeared to be wealthy and to know where he was going. He seemed to be everything I thought I was not. I pursued and eventually married the only man I ever really dated. It didn't take long before he dominated my life, demanding that I adopt his world view—his religion, prejudices and preferences. It was not worth arguing the merits of my taste in food, fun or ideas. There was only one acceptable way of being—his. Ultimately, I neither trusted nor respected him—after his open adulterous affair, chronic unemployment, unethical business deals and outright illegal behavior. Life became one fight after another, one explosion followed by the next. Even then, I would have stayed if he had given any hopeful response to my pleas for a meaningful relationship."

# Choosing a Mate: Life's Single Most Important Challenge

For more than 25 years I have worked with people like Jessica and Barbara—people struggling to make their marriages successful. I have encountered couples with nearly every kind of relationship, and over time I have developed a whole set of conclusions about what determines the degree of happiness in a marriage.

At the top of my list is this one: *Your choice of whom to marry is more crucial than everything else combined that you will ever do to make your marriage succeed.* If you choose wisely, your life will be significantly easier and infinitely more satisfying. But if you make a serious mistake, your marriage may fail, causing you and perhaps your children immeasurable pain. Most of the failed marriages I have encountered were in trouble the day they began. The two people involved simply chose the wrong person to marry.

## Is There Skill Involved in Mate Selection?

Why do some individuals choose their "lifelong" partners so poorly? Because they have received almost no instruction about how to do it well. And how in the world are you supposed to make such a brilliant choice when you have been "coached" so little?

So much of the coaching that does exist is outrageously superficial and ultimately destructive. For instance, Margaret Kent's 1987 best-selling book *How to Marry the Man of Your Choice* proudly boasts, "This book examines the techniques of manipulation. You will learn how to manipulate others, and how to prevent others from manipulating you." Kent tells women the 20 places to look for a man; how "criticisms can make him fall in love with you"; and how to develop their own "sales pitch." She claims her book will "guide you to the altar—regardless of your looks, your past, your age!" [1]

Our society—specifically, television and the movie industry—teaches people to rely almost exclusively on their "natural instincts" when choosing a mate. But romantic feelings, those seemingly trustworthy emotions, offer almost nothing of substance when it comes to making a wise choice about a potential marriage partner. In fact, they frequently get in the way. They literally anesthetize you to the critical factors you desperately need to examine.

But here's the good news: *Choosing a marriage partner successfully is a skill you can develop.*

The central theme of this book is that you can make a wise decision about the person you marry. Great marriages are possible if you select a great mate, and this selection is virtually never the consequence of luck or laziness. It is the reward given to those who follow carefully formulated principles. Those who adhere to these principles may not always be aware that they are doing so. But if they end up with a marriage partner they can love and live with happily for a lifetime, I guarantee that the concepts in this book played a crucial role. If you know these principles up front and learn to practice them conscientiously, you can significantly increase the probability of having a great marriage. But if you count on luck and chance—or passion and romance—there is a better than 50 percent probability that your marriage will be disappointing, if not excruciatingly painful.

# *Love Can Turn Sour*

Each year in the United States, more than 200,000 marriages end prior to the couples' *second* anniversary. Imagine the collective pain of these 400,000 people!

But as overwhelmingly painful as these breakups are, they may represent far and away the least devastating of all the divorces—if the couple has no children. It is when children become involved that pain begins to multiply.

In her 1991 book *When the Bough Breaks*, Sylvia Ann Hewlett explores the massive consequences of the breakdown of the American family. She points to divorce and illegitimacy rates that are almost beyond comprehension.[2] According to one estimate, a white child born in the early 1980s will have only a 30 percent chance of living to age 17 with both biological parents at home, and a black child has just a 6 percent chance.[3]

We cannot fail to recognize that such chaos in the fundamental unit of our society is responsible for much of the agony people are experiencing today.

When our system of nurturing has reached this level of decay, we can expect all manner of frantic behavior, from gangs and drugs to mental breakdowns and suicide.

## Marriage Can Be Magnificent

There is good news, however. Marriage can be wonderful!

Nothing in life can rival the experience of a man and woman in love and a family grounded in the commitment of their parents. It's enormously appealing to share life at the deepest levels with someone to whom you are more attracted than anyone else in the world. It is the sense of being in partnership with a person who likes the things you like, thinks the way you think, works as hard to make your marriage succeed as you do, and who, above all else, thoroughly loves you and contributes to your growth and self-esteem. When you find a person like this, your dream of experiencing deep happiness and total fulfillment is well within your grasp.

But it all begins with you and your dedication to making a prudent decision. And however gloomy the statistics about marriage seem to be, your choice of a partner can be made more wisely and skillfully than was true for your parents or grandparents. The 10 principles of this book are a distillation of the most recent scientific research and the most durable ancient teachings. If you steadfastly follow these principles, you will have a significantly better chance of making a wise decision about the person you marry and forging a lasting and deeply satisfying relationship.

## We Seek a Revolution

What we desperately need in America is a revolution—a total change in our mate-selection procedures. That's what this book is about!

I strongly believe that we can significantly improve this vital area of our corporate life. Men and women throughout our land can be helped to find a person to love with whom they can experience a lifetime of meaning. It takes hard work and patience. It requires training and guidance. But after all, it is for a lifetime. It is worth every ounce of time and effort you give it.

So let the revolution begin with you. No more second-rate marriages! Great marriages—that must be our goal.

# ONE
# Eliminate the Seven Most Prevalent Causes of Faulty Mate Selection

After spending the weekend in San Diego, some colleagues and I headed back to Los Angeles on the I-5 freeway. A few miles north of San Diego there is a checkpoint where the U.S. Immigration and Naturalization Service tries to spot cars hiding illegal aliens and transporting them across the border from Mexico to the United States.

Signs along the freeway instruct drivers to stay in their own lane and slow down. Thousands of cars comply, and the traffic backs up for miles. When you finally come to the checkpoint, there is a uniformed agent in each lane, carefully scanning every car. He waves almost all of the cars through, stopping one to be checked only now and then. Once past this point, drivers speed on down the highway.

When our car reached the agent, he looked us over and waved us on. As we sped toward Los Angeles, we mused about the officer: "What does he look for? What are the clues he has learned to trust? What raises his suspicion? How can he know so quickly whether there is a problem or not?" You can imagine the theories a carload of psychologists came up with!

Later I realized my office is kind of like that checkpoint on the freeway. One young couple after another—all contemplating marriage—comes through, and I sometimes "pull them over" and look more closely when I fear their partnership is in real danger.

I certainly am fooled now and then. I met for seven premarital sessions with one couple about four years ago. I felt absolutely sure that they were nearly perfect for one another. A year later, they were separated, and now they are divorced. But I'm not fooled very often. After all these years of working with hundreds of couples and then keeping up with many of them after their marriages, I'm convinced that my accuracy rate is high.

So I asked myself what I look for when it comes to danger signals. I've always known that the strengths of a relationship are far more obvious than the signs of impending failure. These latter clues are often as invisible as cancer in a body. They hide and move and make detection difficult.

With couples, it is love that sometimes masks the very defects that can kill a marriage as systematically as cancer destroys a body. When malignant cells invade the body of a tanned, robust young person, how in the world are you supposed to suspect a disease is at work? And when two young people come bouncing into my office, full of romance and excitement, how do I know whether this relationship is likely to experience some serious problems?

Researchers have learned to pick up on these problems so effectively that one recent study indicates marital success or failure can now be predicted before the wedding day with 81 percent accuracy. From this research and my own 25 years of experience, I have formulated a seven-point checklist for faulty mate selection.

## *1. The Decision to Get Married Is Made Too Quickly.*

If there is anything that catches my attention, it's two people telling me they have known each other for a couple of months, and now they're ready to pledge themselves to each other for the rest of their lives. I want to say: "*What?* Do you know what 'the rest of your lives' means? It means thousands of breakfasts together, going through all kinds of financial crises together, enduring sickness or depression, facing heavy disappointments together, maybe even watching each other get old and lose physical control. And you think you're ready to make this kind of decision after only a few days or weeks or months?"

Of course, I'm usually able to keep all this intensity to myself, but they get my point. When a couple is ready to decide on something as all-encompassing as marriage after only a few weeks or months of dating, I assume their decision is long on fantasy and short on reality. It is an indication to me that the "task" of marriage is being seriously underestimated, that the maturity it takes to make a marriage successful year in and year out has not yet been developed.

I have read thousands of pages about mate selection, mostly research studies of one kind or another, and I have worked with hundreds of couples contemplating marriage. I have counseled even more who were married and in serious trouble. I am absolutely convinced that when the decision to marry is made too quickly, it places the partnership at tremendous risk.

A few years ago, an empirical study by researchers at Kansas State University was published that underscores the importance of spending plenty of time together prior to marriage. In their sample of 51 middle-aged wives, "a strong correlation was found between length of time spent dating their current spouses and current marital satisfaction." These researchers noted that marriage after relatively short dating periods sometimes has positive results, but longer periods provide more experience in potentially troublesome areas. This research found that "couples who had dated for more than two years scored consistently high on marital satisfaction, while couples who had dated for shorter periods scored in a wide range from very high to very low."[1] Thus, the risk of marital failure is significantly reduced by longer dating periods.

I'm every bit as concerned about hurry-up *second* marriages—sometimes even more so. The possibility of a rebound effect is enormous.

I know a number of people in their second marriage, and if these "second chances" turn out well, it's usually because the people involved took their time. One community leader wrote: "My second marriage benefited greatly from the lessons I learned as a result of my first marriage. The smartest thing I did was wait four years to remarry so I was able to accept my responsibility for what went wrong in the first marriage."

It isn't just divorcees and widows who jump into marriage. The loss of a significant dating relationship or engagement can send one searching for a replacement. Sometimes it has to do with feelings of rejection, low self-esteem or loneliness. And sometimes, people hurry into new marriages to shortcut their grief process. This was the case with a friend who wrote to me recently:

> The selection process involving my wife was confusing to say the least. I was 24 when I met Patti. I was reeling from the death of my fiancée who had died in an auto accident only a month before. I didn't realize I was avoiding the grief and pain of my loss. I felt God had allowed my life to follow this path and I should just get on with it. I dated Patti once before leaving Chicago to live in Boston. I thought she was a good person, and I corresponded with her for about four months. I didn't know her well, but I impulsively asked her to marry me six months after I had met her. There was little, if any, thought about whether this was a good selection. I figured we would 'work it out.' I tried to make myself believe I was not marrying on the rebound.

This marriage probably never had a chance. It didn't die suddenly, but it died inevitably. This friend learned a painful lesson about hurrying into marriage.

It is a fact that choosing a mate for life is much more complex than the movies make it out to be. The prospect of marriage must be looked at from many angles, analyzed in good times and bad, evaluated for its longevity as well as its early excitement. I don't want to be unrealistic, but I am convinced that when people take two or three years to consider the quality of their partnership, they have a significantly better likelihood of making a wise and accurate choice.

With this kind of crucial, life-changing decision, you need to be patient and thorough in collecting the important data. Take your time! It is much, much easier getting into a relationship than living through years and years of a painful, unfulfilling one.

## 2. *The Decision Is Made at Too Young an Age.*

When two recent high school graduates come to me and declare their plans to marry, my brain immediately flashes *Danger*. I know the divorce rate for couples under 20 is incredibly high. Social scientists have found that people who marry young are seldom prepared for marital roles.

As a matter of fact, the divorce rate for 21- and 22-year-olds is twice as high as it is for 24- and 25-year-olds.

When our oldest daughter, Lorrie, was 16 and dreaming of going to UCLA, I often went to her room in the evening just to talk. One night, I "preached" to her the "absolute necessity" of waiting to get married until she was old enough to really know herself and what she needed in a husband. "Lorrie," I said, "I want you to wait until you're 24 to get married." There was a little pause, and then she said in a very calm, quiet voice, "I will, Dad."

I was convinced she wasn't mature enough to know what she was "promising" me, and so I paced a little and presented her with a few more arguments designed to inoculate her against the perils of early marriage. "But

Lorrie," I protested, "I just *know* what's going to happen. You're going to go to UCLA, and all those boys are going to fall in love with you. They're going to want to marry you right away, and they're going to pressure you to get married—however old you are." She paused again, looked me long and hard right in the eye, and repeated her intention with the same calm voice, "I plan to wait, Dad."

Later, when I was discussing all this with Dr. James Dobson on the "Focus on the Family" radio program, I admitted that the years went by and Lorrie stuck by her promise. She got to be 24, and then she was 25. All of a sudden it occurred to me that maybe she thought I said 34. Suddenly, my fears turned in the opposite direction, and I thought, *When is she going to get married?* I needn't have been worried, however, since she and Greg were married shortly thereafter.

Why was I so concerned about Lorrie getting married too early? The theory goes like this: Young people can't select a marriage partner very effectively if they don't know themselves well. In this society, where adolescence often lasts until the middle 20s, identity formation is incomplete until individuals have emotionally separated from their parents and discovered the details of their own uniqueness. Prior to their mid-20s, young adults haven't defined their goals and needs. They haven't had time to learn to be independent. They aren't in a good position to know the kind of person with whom they could form a meaningful lifelong attachment. They simply need more life experience.

How old should two people be when they marry? That all depends on a lot of different factors—maturity level, ability to earn a living, progress in education and so on. But we can say for sure that, statistically, marriages seem to be much more stable when they begin no earlier than the mid-20s. As a matter of fact, a recent study indicates that the most stable marriages of all have a "starting date" of 28 years of age.

Lest you think I'm out of touch with reality, I need to tell you that even in 1890, the average age of American males at first marriage was slightly over

26 years. The median age for females in 1890 was 22 years. Through the years, these averages gradually declined to 22.8 for males and 20.3 for females after the second world war in 1950. But by 1988 the average age for men at first marriage was back up to 25.9, and the average age for women had reached an all-time high of 23.6. The average age at marriage for females is higher now than at any time in our history, and there is a slow, upward trend.

Marcia and Tom Lasswell are two sociologists whose work has strongly influenced my own thinking. In 1974, Marcia Lasswell wrote an article entitled "Is There a Best Age to Marry? An Interpretation." She concluded:

> Divorce rates are lowest for both men and women who marry for the first time at age 28 or later. The chances for a stable marriage increase as both partners reach the age of 30 and then the rates level off. Couples who desire children have reason not to wait much beyond ages 30 to 35 to marry if they want to have children before the risk factor of late pregnancy becomes an issue. This knowledge has led to the conclusion that the maximum likelihood of success in companionship, affection and procreation in marriage exists when marriage occurs between the ages of 28 and 34 (allowing a year for conception if one child is planned), between 28 and 32 if two children are planned, and between 28 and 30 if three children are planned. If no children are desired, the age of the couple for parenthood obviously is not a consideration. [2]

If you want to eliminate one of the most prevalent causes of marriage failure, take seriously the need to wait until you have personally developed your identity and life goals. If you do, your selection of a mate will be based on the "totally grown up you" and prove to be as good 10 or 20 years from now as it is today.

## 3. One or Both Persons Are Too Eager to Be Married.

Even though it was 10 years ago, I remember very well when Rick and Sally came to me for premarital counseling. I had known Rick from a distance for a long time, because his parents lived in the same town where I grew up. But I had never met Sally until I saw her in my waiting room.

Rick was a terrific guy, and all the younger children in town idolized him. He had a caring friendliness that kids trusted, and he had a reputation for being one of the nicest guys around. Sally was very good looking, serious, organized and to the point. She was clearly in charge, always answered first when I asked them questions, and she corrected Rick several times as he related his experiences.

Rick came from a great home, and even though he had not dated very much, I got the feeling he was emotionally healthy and well put together. Sally's parents were divorced; her dad had moved when she was 12, and she had not seen him often since. Her mother was the first woman to be promoted to executive vice president of the major bank where she worked. She was clearly a hardworking, powerful woman who, though she traveled a lot, took a big interest in Sally and her younger sister. Throughout Sally's adolescence, her mom was involved in a time-consuming relationship, and her work responsibilities and stress grew steadily. She spent less and less time at home and demanded more from Sally and her sister to maintain control of the household. On the one hand, Sally was lonely, but she was also chafing to get out of the house. She was eager to leave her mother's ironfisted authority.

What's more, three and a half months earlier Sally had experienced the rejection of her longtime boyfriend, whom she had dated through several years of high school and college. She had lost herself in that relationship through the years of loneliness when her mother's job and outside relationships had taken her away from home. Sally panicked when her boyfriend said that he thought they needed to be apart and he wanted to take out other girls. She felt totally alone, lost really, and she began to grope for security.

Rick and Sally worked at the same large clothing store, and they had been acquainted for several months. Rick was friendly with virtually everyone, but his shyness kept him from getting involved in much dating. So when Sally made her move, Rick was willing. Before he knew what had happened, he was in my office for premarital counseling.

I put Rick and Sally through the usual tests and interviews for any couple seeking my assistance. And from the beginning I saw real problems. Their scores on the various personality tests were not very compatible, and they simply didn't agree on a lot of things. More than that, there was a feeling of tension in the air for me. I could put my finger on several concerns, but I couldn't explain all the things I felt.

But here's the point: When I tried to bring up one of my concerns from the tests and interviews, Sally would immediately offer a rationale explaining it away. Rick often indicated a desire to talk more about the concern, apparently recognizing that it was a problem worth discussing. However, when Sally tried to quickly "resolve" and eliminate the problem, Rick always acquiesced. She was too strong. More than that, she was so eager to get married that she wouldn't look objectively at the facts.

It was obvious to me that Sally was deeply committed to leaving behind her loneliness, rejection and feelings of resentment toward both her mother and ex-boyfriend. As far as she was concerned, this marriage to Rick would be fine, and it would substantially reduce the misery she was in. So against my recommendation, they got married.

Only six months later, I heard that they had separated and were heading for divorce. Under the stress of living together, significant problems and differences began to appear.

Eighteen months after that, I saw Rick at an anniversary celebration for one of his cousins. We had a little time to talk, and he was still reeling from what he had been through. It took him two more years to get on with his life, and many years beyond that to really recover.

There are a lot of reasons why people are "too eager" to get married. Sometimes they get worried that their partner will have a change of heart. This worry increases their pulse rate and makes them want to act fast. Or they may be sick and tired of being alone on weekends, and they are convinced that once married they will never have to be alone on a Saturday night again. So they hurry.

Overeagerness to marry is most often associated with the deep and powerful excitement that bubbles up around impending marriage. Sure, marriages are exciting, but when two people become driven by the excitement, they often fail to recognize the heavy demands of marriage. They may press ahead with a choice that won't stand the test of time. They get so excited to "head for Disneyland" that they fail to consider the long-term ramifications of their choice.

Overeagerness is pretty easy to spot. It is clearly one of those causes of marriage failure you want to eliminate from the beginning. A lifetime decision like marriage requires a clear, unhurried mind.

## 4. One or Both May Be Choosing a Mate to Please Someone Else.

Why would anyone select a marriage partner in order to please someone else? On the surface that's a reasonable question, but as a psychologist, I find it easy to answer. Most of us try hard to please others, and some of us establish our whole identity out of our need to make everyone else happy.

I immediately begin to squirm when I realize one member of a couple has chosen his or her partner in order to please a parent or some other important person. I've watched this strategy backfire so many times I can hardly contain myself. It simply won't work! To make a good decision, you must make it in light of *your own* needs and dreams and life objectives . . . not someone else's.

Does that mean you shouldn't take seriously what the important people in your life think about your choice? Of course not. Friends and family know you well, and they want you to be happy. So you should listen carefully to their input and take into consideration what they say. But sometimes other people desire to have you make *them* happy. Even though they don't know you like you know yourself, and even though *you* are the one who will live with your spouse through the years, they essentially want you to let them make the decision.

I often say to people, "Don't let *anyone* select your marriage partner for you, and don't allow yourself to select a lifetime mate in order to satisfy someone else. This is *your* marriage, *your* once-in-a-lifetime opportunity!"

I have found all kinds of "other persons" willing to make the decision for you. Most often it's a parent. Mom and Dad have a way, perhaps because of their life experience, of thinking they can make this decision better than you can. They may be right, but they may be wrong. Whatever the case, it's *your* decision, and if you let someone else take over, you run a severe risk of experiencing long-term resentment.

As a parent, I know what it's like to feel strongly about the partners my children marry. My wife and I have taken an intense interest in the men our daughters have considered. If there is anything parents need to pray about, their children's marriage partner should be at the top of the list. Every child needs all the divine and parental direction possible.

But all my hours of listening to people in the intimate relationship of psychotherapy has taught me one gigantic lesson: Parental influence—even without a word being spoken—is incredibly intense and powerful. However careful a person is, virtually every "child" has a strong tendency to choose a mate because of his parents' encouragement or discouragement.

If parents are smart, they'll recognize all this when the time for choosing comes. They will counsel their children to make the decision on the basis of all the data available, but the choice must be *their own* choice, or there may be terrible trouble ahead. If parents think their children are incapable of considering the data because they are not sufficiently developed personally, or because they are too troubled or conflicted within themselves, it is reasonable to encourage them to seek professional counseling before committing for a lifetime. But when they make their choice, it needs to be their own, a free and independent decision they can live with and own for as long as they live.

One last word on this point to those who are considering this choice: I strongly encourage you to pay close attention to *all* the input that comes to you before you choose. Other people's opinions are important, the teaching you have received is crucial, and the reading you do will be helpful. When you're through with all of that, listen carefully to yourself from deep within. The greatest challenge of your life will be to stand in the middle of all the opinions, information and feelings, and make the wisest decision possible.

Whatever you do, don't jeopardize your life by making a decision just because you don't want to hurt your partner, or because you think your friends might think badly of you, or because the invitations are out, or even because someone older thinks the two of you would be good for each other.

## 5. The Experience Base Is Too Narrow.

Sometimes couples come to me considering a decision about marriage, but their way of knowing one another and being known is just too narrow. It's not necessarily that they haven't dated long enough. They simply have not walked together through the variety of circumstances and situations necessary to really know someone. Perhaps they have had too much of one kind of experience and not nearly enough of other kinds. Here are three examples:

Jim and Nancy had known each other for two years. They met at a wedding, and they went out several times during their first summer together. Jim left in early September to begin his junior year at an eastern college; Nancy left for her sophomore year at SMU in Dallas. They wrote letters to each other all year, and they met at Christmastime in Phoenix, which is Nancy's home and fairly near where Jim grew up. The following summer they were together again, and after two months of dating—sandwiched around their heavy work schedules—they talked about marriage and even made some plans. Then Jim left for his senior year in the East, Mary for her junior year in Dallas, and the letter writing began again. Thankfully, they realized they didn't know each other well enough to feel sure about their decision, so they came to me. They had known each other for more than a year, dated 12 to 15 times and written a lot of letters. But they hadn't been through the ins and outs of daily life enough to know each other deeply.

Bob and Karen have a different story, but the problem is similar. Ever since they met, they've been living on a cloud, floating from one form of ecstasy to another. They are tremendously attracted to one another physically, and they feel wildly in love!

But they haven't ever talked much about other things. They don't really know what the other person likes or dislikes in most areas of life. They haven't spent much time together with their families, and they have never had a single argument.

Couples in this state of starry-eyed bliss are some of the most dangerous and difficult to deal with. They're like an airplane approaching a fluffy cloud mass. The clouds look huge and white and brilliant—but they may be covering a mountain. And catastrophe could lie ahead.

I think you see my point. People who are so "in love" don't usually want to be bothered with "problem talk." They're convinced that they have all the evidence they need to choose one another. But in truth, the narrowness of their experience with each other makes their decision terribly risky.

Finally, there's Fred and Cyndi. They are both deeply involved in their church and have been since they met. Fred works with a junior high group at the church, and he spends hours with them every week. When you stack these responsibilities on top of his full-time job, he's left with little time or energy. Early on, he recruited Cyndi to help him with the group. They have come to know each other largely on the basis of this association. They began "dating," but they hardly ever went out by themselves. They were always planning youth group events, leading camp-outs and spending time with the kids. Obviously, there is nothing wrong with knowing each other this way, but when the *only* interaction is at church, the picture is incomplete. Marriage involves all of life, and Fred and Cyndi have explored only a small part of it.

It's crucial to broaden your experiences together as much as possible. Spend time with your spouse-to-be early in the morning and late at night; in heavy traffic and on country roads; in times of stress and easygoing moments. Observe him or her playing with children, doing household chores and balancing the checkbook.

Too many couples have flown excitedly into the clouds and encountered a mountain of painful problems. But the more experiences you have together, the better your chances of avoiding hidden surprises.

# 6. The Couple Has Unrealistic Expectations.

Just last week a woman came to my office to talk about her failed marriage: "I wonder how something that starts out so full of hope and love can go so wrong. I just knew that once I married him, once he saw what love really was, then everything would be all right. Then he would change and love me back just as much as I loved him. He had it all inside him; he just needed to be loved enough to let it out. I would be the one to open him up. I would be the woman who made life worthwhile for him."

You can probably sense the impracticality of her words, just as I did. It is presumptuous and naive to think you alone can change someone. Unfortunately, this woman found out how unrealistic her expectations were.

Another woman, only two years into her marriage, said: "I never expected all these financial problems. He always seemed to have a lot of money when we were dating. I just assumed there would *never* be money problems." Then there's the couple, on the verge of divorce shortly after the honeymoon, who said: "We had no idea we would have so many areas of disagreement. We can't even agree on what the temperature of our room should be at night."

After hearing stories like these, I echo the words of my favorite sportscaster, Dick Enberg: *"Oh my!"*

I'm reminded of that famous first line of M. Scott Peck's great book *The Road Less Traveled*, "Life is difficult." He's right about that, and if he means that life is difficult for individuals, I'm convinced that it's *twice* as difficult for two people to make a marriage work.

John Welwood wrote a 1990 journal article that I have found extremely helpful. I like his view of expectations:

> If we focus only on the loving side of a relationship, we may become caught in the "bliss trap"—imagining that love is a stairway to heaven that will allow us to rise above the nitty-gritty elements of our personality and leave behind all our fears and limitations: "Love is so fantastic! I feel so high! Let's get married; won't everything be wonderful!" Of course these expansive feelings are wonderful. But the potential distortion here is to imagine that love by itself can solve our problems, provide endless comfort and pleasure, or save us from facing ourselves, our aloneness, our pain, or, ultimately, our death. Becoming too attached to the heavenly side of love leads to rude shocks and disappointments when we inevitably return to earth and have to deal with the real-life challenges of *making a relationship work*. [3]

When a couple, young or not so young, decides to marry, they had better be aware that they're going to face some real difficulties, even if things develop in the most positive way. Making a new relationship work places enormous stress on most people. If couples know that pain and strain are inevitable, they have a significantly better chance of dealing effectively with them. The key is to be aware of what you're getting into so you won't be shocked and turned off to one another.

Our expectations are largely formed by what we observed in our childhood home. If your parents let you in on their own lives together—the disagreements, struggles, joys, milestones—you probably have a fairly realistic picture of married life. But sometimes parents, with the very best intentions, deal with all the tough stuff behind closed doors, or worse yet, they push it down inside themselves. Then their kids develop a sense that marriage is relatively easy.

The truth is, successful marriages require an incredible amount of hard work. You will experience all kinds of pain, and there will be problems all along the way. And however well your marriage turns out, you will still have dozens of personal challenges to test your mettle. To expect anything different is to set your marriage up for trouble.

I have watched many marriages sink because the couples expected life to be filled with ivy-covered cottages, walks on the beach, steamy love scenes and nonstop fun. That's just not reality.

# 7. One or Both May Have Unaddressed Significant Personality or Behavior Problems.

If there are qualities about your partner's personality or behavior that you question—like jealousy, temper, irresponsibility, dishonesty or stubbornness— ask yourself if you're willing to spend the rest of your life dealing with these problems. Personality features like these rarely vanish when you get married. That's why I get so concerned when a couple goes ahead with marriage even though there are significant defects that haven't been resolved.

Most of the problems I named above are personality traits, meaning they happen over and over in many different situations, not just once or twice over a long period of time. If your potential partner was in a bad mood two or three months ago, that's no big deal. But when her mood fluctuates a lot in the same week, and there are too many of those "weeks," you're dealing with an established personality trait.

These difficulties probably started out as strategies designed to handle some part of life. Take lying, for instance. Your potential partner found himself in a tight spot, perhaps early in his life. If he told the truth, he looked bad or lost something of value—like getting to stay up and watch television. So he lied, and when he did, his anxiety about the pain he feared was reduced. This kind of reinforcement makes lying under similar circumstances more likely to occur the next time he faces a dilemma. When these behaviors have been tried over and over with regular reinforcement, they become a habit.

If someone you love is regularly undependable or untruthful or irritable, it will be extremely difficult for you to build trust, let alone enjoy him or her. And if you can't trust or enjoy your partner, look out!

Obviously, if the person you are considering has a drug or drinking problem or trouble with sexual integrity, you should make *absolutely sure* that he or she has worked through the problem well in advance of your marriage. (I'll offer more information for determining problem areas in your potential partner in chapter 4.) Two things will happen if you don't: Your leverage will become decidedly less after you have announced your long-term intentions. That is, your partner will have little motivation to improve behavior once you're married. To make matters worse, the stress of marriage will tend to magnify the problems and make them considerably more difficult to manage over time.

A highly successful businessman told me a few days ago that his marriage is a mess because he ignored an obvious psychological problem he had recognized in his wife long before their wedding day. "She *always* has to have her way," he told me, "and that has been true since I met her. When we were dating and trying to decide which movie to see, she would make her choice and settle for no compromise. Through the years, it has been one thing after another—when we would have children and how many we would have, what we would name them, where we would live, and on and on. There was no major decision she didn't want to make. And I came to see that I had two alternatives: agree with her or call it quits. I hate divorce, and I've refused to give up, but I've lived in misery my entire marriage."

That's a terribly sad story, isn't it? You may wonder if he and his wife tried hard enough to deal with the problem. When I asked him about that, he assured me they had been in counseling three different times. Still, the problem had barely budged through the years.

Do not, under any circumstances, move ahead with marriage until significant personal problems have been addressed and fully overcome. If you do, there is tremendous potential danger for your relationship.

# Summing Up Principle #1

So there they are, the seven most deadly causes of faulty mate selection. If you can eliminate these, you'll significantly increase your chances of building a solid marriage.

You may wonder how many of these seven danger signs you can violate without taking too much of a risk. Unfortunately, the answer is *none*. It is possible that some people can get married after being together only a few weeks and make a success of their marriage. I would never deny that, because I know it has happened. But it's a clear exception to the rule. The same kind of reasoning is valid for the other six problems.

If you follow this first principle, you will be rid of the major causes of choosing the wrong mate. Then you will be free to think more positively about how you can make your marriage wonderfully happy and deeply meaningful by design and careful intention.

The rewards of wise mate selection are overwhelming, and your hard work will pay off. I am always struck with the enormous number of lives that potentially will be affected by every marriage of one man to one woman. For instance, when my mother and father married on that summer day in 1915, who could have known that there would be 45 of us in the family (children and grandchildren) while the two of them were still living—with all of us recognizing that their marriage had significantly influenced our own lives in many ways.

I get excited by the idea that people everywhere can tremendously increase their chances of being happy and providing a healthy environment for their loved ones if they will simply recognize the vital importance of these seven issues.

# TWO
# Develop a Clear Mental Image of Your Ideal Spouse

My wife and I recently held a surprise birthday party for one of our closest friends. During the party, I mingled among the guests like a good host should, and I encountered a wife and husband team who apparently had better social skills than mine. That is, they got me talking about *myself*—instead of me getting them to talk about *themselves*.

I told this couple I was immersed in writing about choosing a marriage partner. They immediately became interested, and they talked briefly about the way they selected each other. A few days later, we received a note from the wife thanking us for the party. She also included a bit more about how she and her husband got together:

> It does all seem like a miracle, especially when I consider that I met Lou on the steps of the Huntington Hotel when I was on a blind date with his Navy roommate. Lou was with an old high school friend. My date was a nice Navy fellow, but Lou was the one for me. Such good intuition—or something. I wonder how we just knew?

I can't tell you how many people I've encountered who "just knew" they had found the right person to marry. When these people reflect carefully on their meeting, they end up assuming it was *intuition*. But I'm puzzled. When the marriage works out successfully, is it because of good intuition? And when the relationship breaks down and the marriage turns sour, is it because of faulty intuition?

The truth is, I don't really believe in intuition. After all these years of listening to people in psychotherapy and analyzing them from every conceivable angle, I've concluded that *intuition* is a word we use when we can't figure out what created an inner sense of "just knowing." However, intuition gives you a sense of magic or something that is part of your inner being quite by chance. Nothing could be further from the truth.

The fact is, what we call intuition is really "unconscious processes" over which we have never taken full conscious control. That's the problem! These below-the-surface thoughts and feelings are often poorly formed and simply untrustworthy. There are too many ways they can be influenced, too many wild and irrational forces that can bend and twist them, and thereby lead us astray. A dominant theme in this book is that a monumental decision like marriage deserves highly precise reasoning. It's crucial to make a rational, proactive, fully conscious decision about the type of person you want to marry. Relying on a vague kind of intuition may be the best explanation for the high rate of divorce in our culture.

# The Psychology of Attraction

Virtually every human being has some kind of "image" in their brain of the kind of person they would like to marry. However, most people keep this image out of consciousness, just beyond awareness. In this unconscious state, these images are difficult to understand and nearly impossible to alter. Nevertheless, they are powerful! They direct us to certain kinds of people, and then we automatically compare them with the image we carry in our heads. Our inner computers discard those "prospects" who do not compare favorably, and tell us to pursue the few who do.

This has probably happened to you. Maybe you went to a party and met several interesting and attractive people. As you mingled and got to know them better, some moved up on your interest scale, and others moved down. Why? What makes some members of the opposite sex become more or less attractive as you get to know them? Of course, it could be obvious factors like foul language or an abrasive personality. Most often, though, it's the degree of "match" between your subconscious image and the other person that filters out the winners and losers.

So how are these images formed? There are three primary theories:

**1.** The perfect mate in our heads is like our parent of the opposite sex. When I was young, I often sang "I want a girl just like the girl who married dear old Dad." I suppose at some time most boys have admired their mother's attributes and girls have idolized their father. However, there is very little empirical research supporting this theory. In fact, one recent study concluded that both boys and girls are most influenced by their mothers when it comes to determining the type of person they will marry.

**2.** The image is fueled by unmet childhood needs from the opposite-sex parent. This theory suggests we seek a mate who will help us meet those needs—such as nurturing, affection, spontaneity—that were never met by our opposite-sex parent.

Harville Hendrix' excellent book *Getting the Love You Want* takes this approach. Even though the research evidence is scanty, he makes a cogent case for the theory:

> The part of your brain that directed your search for a mate ... was trying to ... re-create the conditions of your upbringing, in order to correct them. ... It was attempting to return to the scene of your original frustration so that you could resolve your unfinished business.[1]

Our powers of observation are especially acute when we are looking for a mate, because we are searching for someone to satisfy our fundamental unconscious drives. We subject everyone to the same intense scrutiny: Is this someone who will nurture me and help me recover my lost self? [2]

**3.** Every child is influenced by countless persons, and each helps shape the image of the desired mate. (This is the theory I favor.) Your parents, relatives, teachers, coaches and others all had certain qualities you found attractive. And each of these qualities became a piece of the puzzle in the formation of your perfect-spouse image.

## *Images Tend to Remain Unconscious*

Why exactly do these images most often stay beyond our consciousness? I think the main reason is fear. Choosing a marriage partner is frightening, because many factors are beyond our control. We may find an ideal mate, but that near-perfect person may not find us ideal. And a high percentage of people have experienced painful rejection from someone they deeply wanted to marry. Thus, we may keep the image of our ideal spouse a secret from even ourselves out of fear that we will be bitterly disappointed. We would rather not even think about our "perfect person" because of the rejection anxiety it produces in us.

Another reason for keeping this image away from our awareness is because we are ashamed of it. It involves so much about us that is deeply personal and intimate. For instance, if you want someone who will nurture you when you're sick or afraid—just the way Mom used to—that might be hard to admit. If you like strong, aggressive men—even though you hate the way Dad used to verbally abuse your mother—it may be hard to reconcile your contradictory feelings. Or if you are looking for someone with a lot of self-confidence, the fact that your own self-esteem is sometimes low may make you feel that your dreams are unreasonable.

The final explanation for why we don't allow our image of the perfect person into consciousness may be the most accurate of all. It's because we are too uncertain about that image. We are aware on some level that our lack of understanding about ourselves severely limits our ability to form a clear image of a good mate. Most of us never had anyone help us think through the kind of person we are and the kind of mate with whom we could be most successful. We are aware of what a crucial selection this is, but we feel undeveloped in this area. Therefore, we keep the unfinished image out of our line of conscious vision.

Maybe all of these explanations have value—but one thing is for sure: Most people can better tell you whether a particular person seems right than they can tell you what "right" is. There must be an image under there somewhere informing the quick judgments they can make about the "rightness" or "wrongness" of a given candidate.

## *"The Person of My Dreams" Versus "The Person I Can Attract"*

All of us know at some level that we can't attract just anyone we want. We all vary when it comes to physical attractiveness, intelligence, education, spiritual vitality, interpersonal skills, financial prospects, and so on. As hard as it is to accept, the people we can actually attract may be much different from those we dream about. It's self-defeating to pretend these realities don't exist.

I saw a cartoon the other day entitled "Single Slices" by Peter Kohlsaat. It shows a middle-aged man reading a newspaper want ad. The particular ad he's reading says: "Incredibly rich and attractive, physically fit natural blonde, Ph.D., M.D., D.V.M., Pulitzer Prize fiction winner, gourmet chef, multilingual, enjoys fishing, watching softball, automechanics and pool—seeks average male 20-75 to share innermost emotions. Need not be good looking or financially secure." At the bottom of the cartoon in large type it simply says: "Truth in advertising does not apply to personal ads."

Obviously, what this cartoon says so powerfully is that persons with an abundance of attributes are not likely to seek mates who have far fewer attractive attributes.

The fact is, some people are going to have more choice about the person they marry than other people. They are genetically endowed with more attractive characteristics. Unfair as it may seem, admirable attributes are not distributed equally among all men and women. I'm sure you know someone who seems to have all the best qualities—intelligence, good looks, athletic prowess, quick wit and charisma.

Other people have all the advantages when it comes to the emotional stability of the home in which they grew up. They may have had emotionally healthy parents, a close family atmosphere, plenty of love, adequate financial resources, and constant encouragement to do their best. A background like this gives people a lot of benefits (self-esteem, educational opportunities, social refinement) that others may not have.

If you are from a divorced, abusive or conflict-ridden home, you may well have developed in ways that put you at a disadvantage when it comes to attracting a person of the opposite sex. This may be because of low self-esteem, fear of intimacy, unresolved anger or any number of problems.

But there are two crucial things I need to point out before you assume there's nothing you can do about your background. First, the person you *can* become is far more important than the person you are today. I think a big part of life is trying to realize your potential as fully as possible. When you start with who you are today and commit yourself to moving steadily toward goals, the progress you experience will not only make you feel genuinely proud, but it will also make you significantly more attractive to members of the opposite sex. If you are hindered by problems that stem from your upbringing, commit to working through them and fulfilling your potential.

This kind of emotional growth is best achieved when you start with a deep understanding that you are totally lovable just the way you are. If your pursuit of excellence grows out of an appreciation for the way you have been created, you'll grow by leaps and bounds. But if you think you must be different to be loved, your anxiety will mount and your growth will be retarded. You *are* lovable! And you *can* actualize more of your potential than you have.

Second, how attractive you are to the opposite sex does not depend on any single quality. Rather, your attractiveness depends on the *sum total* of all your qualities. Your strengths may balance out your weaknesses. A high score on one quality like "personality" can compensate for a lower score on another quality like "good looks." The trick is to *maximize* your strengths and *minimize* your weaknesses. For instance, if you feel like your social skills are deficient, there are all kinds of ways to improve them. Read books on the subject, take a class or talk to friends you admire.

Also, realize that different people of the opposite sex will rate you differently on each quality. Some people are strongly attracted by a good sense of humor, others like career ambition and still others see spiritual depth as most important.

So my challenge to you is to become all that you are capable of becoming. At the same time I encourage you to look squarely at yourself and appraise your overall attractiveness accurately. But remember this: It's probably best to search for someone who seems to be a little above you—and then to try with all you have to become the person who will be attractive to that individual.

# *What Specifically Do You Want in a Mate?*

Marcia and Thomas Lasswell have honed in on the subject of attraction this way:

> George Bernard Shaw . . . once commented that love is an overemphasis on the difference between one person and all others.

Once we have discovered that all people are not alike, we begin to have different feelings about different individuals. We feel 'better,' 'happier' or 'more powerful' in the presence of some people than in the presence of others. We wish to spend more time with some and less time (or perhaps none at all) with others. We can actually sense changes in our bodies when particular people are near us. Since at some point relationships involve attraction between two people, it is important to understand this phenomenon.[3]

It's crucial to clarify your image of the person to whom you wish to be attracted. I've identified 10 general dimensions that are important to consider while formulating the image of your ideal spouse. You may choose to add to this list, but these are the dimensions most often considered. First, think through the specific qualities from each of these areas that describe your perfect mate. Then rank these 10 areas (from most important to least important) so you know which ones are essential to you. When you've finished these tasks, you should have a clear picture of the "ideal person" with whom you would like to spend the rest of your life.

# *Personality*

What type of personality do you want your future mate to have? Here are five questions to get you thinking:

1. Would you like your mate to be quiet and somewhat shy, or talkative and gregarious?

2. Do you prefer people who are intense and logical, or laid-back and easygoing?

3. Are you most drawn to people who are funny or serious?

4. Would you like someone who is strong and independent, or someone who leaves the decision making up to you?

5. Do you prefer softness or toughness—that is, someone who is gentle and seldom shows signs of anger, or someone who says exactly what he or she thinks and feels?

As many different personalities as there are in the world, there is someone who will match up well with each of them. The crucial thing is not to seek after someone whose personality is like your father's or mother's—but to search for that person whose personality would make you genuinely happy through the years.

My dad was a strong, independent man. He grew up with a forceful, dominant mother, and her children seemed to pick up her traits rather than their father's softer, gentler qualities. What my dad needed in a spouse was someone who could accommodate his strong opinions and take-charge style, someone who could harmonize with his personality. Fortunately for both of them—and my two sisters and me—my mother's personality blended well with my father's.

My parents knew themselves well enough to understand what they needed in a spouse. And that should be true for you, since mate selection depends heavily on knowing yourself well. You are not looking for someone who might be voted "Mate of the Year" by the general public or by your friends. You need to choose someone with a personality *you* can live with and enjoy.

# *Intelligence*

No one wants to marry someone well below them in intelligence. But you may not want to marry a genius either. The fact is, many people with very high IQs have a hard time relating socially.

When I was in graduate school, I spent many Saturdays testing would-be pilots for major airlines. We gave these candidates all kinds of technical and general tests to determine whether they would be good pilots. One of the fascinating parts I remember related to a "correction factor" we applied for some correct answers on a "general information" test. Researchers had discovered that the best pilots weren't necessarily the ones who knew the most, so in order to choose the ideal pilots we lowered the scores of those who knew too much. Their knowledge of a lot of general information meant they were too broadly trained and not specifically suited to the specialized tasks involved in being a pilot.

Sometimes, a potential mate is too intelligent. Or maybe he is smart in ways that make him a bad match for you. What kind of intelligence do you want your future mate to have? Recent studies indicate that in stable marriages there is a high correlation in intelligence. That is, couples do best when they are matched with someone similar—whether they are both geniuses, average or below average.

What *kind* of intelligence would you like in your mate—analytical or intuitive? Do you prefer a "thinker" or a "feeler"? Do you like to go to movies with someone who analyzes what the movie was trying to say or someone who talks about how the movie made him or her *feel*?

Keep in mind that there are different types of intelligence. Some people have incredible memory and can retain facts about everything. Other people have a high aptitude for languages, like my friend Bob Larson. He can speak five or six languages fluently—while I'm hard pressed to remember 50 words from my two years of college French. Still others can conceptualize and visualize schematics. Our middle daughter, Luann, showed this kind of intelligence at a very young age. She could assemble various contraptions by following directions that her 30-year-old father couldn't understand.

The point is, people possess various *types* of intelligence as well as various *degrees* of intelligence. I'm suggesting you figure out the level and type of intelligence you want your mate to have.

# *Appearance*

When it comes to forming an image of the ideal mate, television promotes *appearance* more than any other quality. Have you noticed that? How a person looks and dresses are portrayed as all-important.

It is suggested that love is automatic between two people if they both satisfy all the appearance criteria. You need to dress in the most fashionable ways, fix your hair according to current styles and drive a red sports car.

In 1986, researcher Stanley Woll studied how clients of a computer dating service selected videotapes to view for prospective dates. The men and women read through autobiographical profiles, and they were asked to think out loud about the factors—age, attractiveness, occupation, hobbies, etc.—they considered in deciding whether or not to view a person's videotape. Age and attractiveness were by far the most frequently mentioned factors in subjects' decision strategies. [4]

While it would be foolish to base your decision too heavily on appearance, your individual tastes should be considered when formulating the image of your perfect person. You must settle on your *own* preferences regarding height, weight, facial appearance, hair color, style of dress, cleanliness and physical movement.

When I was an adolescent, it was assumed that in dating relationships the boy would always be taller than the girl, and this principle was virtually never violated. Today, it's not uncommon to see a tall woman with a short man. Does the man being taller than the woman matter to you?

In our culture there is a premium placed on being the "right weight" for your height—not too thin and not too heavy. If there is a bias, it's toward thin women and "solid" or strong men. But other cultures promote different weight ideals. My colleague and friend Dr. Angela Rose is Greek. When she was growing up, her family lived in Los Angeles but spent their summers in Greece. In the United States, she was considered physically fit, but in Greece everyone said she was too skinny.

The point is, standards of appearance vary from culture to culture, region to region, and individual to individual. Try to separate your tastes from those presented by the popular media. Determine a look you will be pleased with.

# *Ambition*

I have counseled several couples for whom significant differences in ambition became the "killer issue." It is absolutely vital that two people have about the same amount of ambition if their marriage is to endure.

I recall a couple I counseled several years ago who struggled with this issue. Jan was the daughter of a prominent politician who had been remarkably successful both in business and politics. Ron was a bright and carefree equipment salesman. He did well but could have done significantly better if he hadn't been so absorbed with sports, particularly golf. He often quit work at two or three in the afternoon to play 18 holes, content to make enough to pay the bills and pursue his hobbies. There was no way he would ever achieve the success Jan was used to—at least not at his present pace.

Jan, on the other hand, was already a vice president of a company her dad had started. She put in 10 to 12 hours every day and often took work home in the evenings. She dreamed of staying home with the children someday, but that would be possible only if Ron would develop the same commitment to work that she had. Ron didn't argue the point with her, except to say he expected to do better through the years and he wished Jan would relax and enjoy life.

Jan finally decided to marry Ron, even though the ambition issue remained a conflict for them. In the middle of their honeymoon, things began to fall apart. A call came saying that Ron's life insurance was going to expire if a payment wasn't sent by Federal Express. He explained that he was having a slow month in sales, and he hadn't been able to cover all his bills. Jan sent the payment out of her account. When they got home, more past-due notices started showing up. All Jan could think of were those afternoons that Ron hadn't worked.

Then things got worse. Ron was unexpectedly laid off. So Jan went to work every day while Ron stayed home to check the want ads, make a few calls and play a round of golf. When several weeks went by without any decent job offers, Jan called me. By this time, their marriage was in deep trouble.

It wasn't as though Ron was unemployable or terribly irresponsible— although that may be a matter of opinion. From my perspective, the critical problem involved career drive and the desire to advance. Ron and Jan simply had different—*very* different—levels of ambition. And though they stayed married, that issue continued to plague them.

It's fine if two people want carefree, relaxing lives. *But they need to be in agreement.* On the other hand, if they want a big house, expensive cars and international trips, they both need to agree on the career styles that will accommodate these aims.

When spouses have different amounts of inner drive, it can cause intense frustration and conflict. But when their levels of ambition are similar, it can bond them together as they strive to reach their goals and achieve their dreams.

# *Chemistry*

My wife and I had some close friends over the other night, a couple we have known for a long time. They told us they were best friends in college for three or four years before they really thought about their relationship in a romantic way. They *liked* each other long before they *loved* each other.

What they were saying, I think, was that "chemistry" played a very small role in their coming together. They didn't *have* to be together because they were so physically drawn to one another. They didn't have a strong drive to stare into each other's eyes or an overpowering urge to touch one another. They spent time together because they had common interests and similar values. Eventually, however, their feelings grew, and they realized their friendship could turn into a great marriage.

Although many people, like these friends, don't feel emotional sparks at first, I believe attraction is critical for long-term satisfaction in marriage. What do you think? Is the magic of romance important to you? Or are you content to make a logical decision based on sound reasoning? How much emphasis do you place on romance and physical attraction? On the basis of what you know about chemistry, does it strike you as an essential factor in the selection of your mate? Is it a major part of the image you have of your perfect person? (We'll examine this topic more thoroughly in chapter 5.)

# *Spirituality*

Research has consistently shown that religious commitment and marital success are highly related.[5] Having a similar religious background is important to marriage because of the traditions and customs the partners will have in common. But I want to make it clear that I'm not just talking about religion here. For me, *spirituality* is a term with substantially more depth than religion.

The dictionary lists 12 different meanings for the word *spirituality*, so I should explain precisely what I mean by it. Religion often refers to *externals*—which church you attend, what denomination you're affiliated with, what traditions you follow. Spirituality refers to *internal* faith and beliefs that run deep.

Spiritual people pay attention to their inner life and understand that there's much more to life than what they see and feel. They look within themselves for the answers that others often seek outside themselves. They are usually committed to meditating or praying regularly. They have a relationship with God, and this relationship often becomes the central part of their existence.

Is it important to you that your mate be spiritually oriented? What if you and your spouse-to-be have different spiritual orientations?

I met with a couple recently for whom spirituality was a source of great tension. The husband has no interest in spiritual matters, while his wife's beliefs are a fundamental part of her life. When she encounters a serious problem, she goes away by herself and seeks answers through prayer. Conversely, the man is convinced that problems are best managed through rational thought and problem solving. This issue causes a lot of conflicts for this couple, because their views are diametrically opposed on a highly sensitive and important issue.

I urge you to evaluate very carefully the spiritual dynamics you're looking for in a mate.

# *Character*

I got a call from a man the other day, and he could barely talk without crying. He had just confirmed what he feared most—his wife was having an affair with his business partner and longtime friend. Both of them had repeatedly lied to him through the months. Now he was devastated; he wondered what there was to live for.

Stories like this are common. Scores of couples have been destroyed because of one person's lying, cheating, irresponsibility, disrespect or slothfulness. I have testified in court about the character makeup of many people, and I have come to believe that the sturdiness and consistency of people's character is a fundamental prerequisite for a stable, long-lasting, joyful marriage.

How important is it to you that your mate be absolutely trustworthy? How hard would it be for you to find that you had been lied to repeatedly? How much do you want to be married to someone who operates on the basis of strongly held values and acts with courage even when it requires sacrifice? How much do you need a mate who absolutely will not cheat for any reason? And how crucial is it that your mate would never steal, act irresponsibly or take drugs?

# *Creativity*

The other night, I watched our daughter, Lindsay, preparing a scrapbook for her closest friend. She was preserving the priceless memories she and this friend had accumulated during their two years in Philadelphia, where they did graduate work at the University of Pennsylvania. She carefully selected all the pictures, arranged them artfully on the pages and wrote out captions to remind them of great moments. Then she decorated the scrapbook with original art work. Nobody had assigned Lindsay that task; nobody even knew she was doing it. It was one of her ways of contributing to their friendship and demonstrating her love.

It isn't only artists, poets and musicians who express their creativity. Abraham Maslow, a great American psychologist, pointed out that creativity happens most often among ordinary folks. When genuine love is mixed with creativity, the lovers can fully celebrate and enjoy their life together.

How does creativity in love and life rank among the other nine traits listed in this chapter?

I know a woman who seems to be one of the world's great mothers. She sings to her little boy and teaches him the songs. She reads book after book to him, plays every kind of game with him, and she has taught him about life in a profound way. But she's not much for keeping the house. The windows often need washing and the garden is overgrown. And sometimes her meals are less than balanced. But when it comes to mothering that boy, she is a creative genius. How would you feel about your mate being like this? How would you feel if the person you marry is creative but falls a little short in other ways?

# *Parenting*

I told my wife the other night that one of the attributes I value most in her is her ability to relate to our three daughters. Through the years she has demonstrated her total loyalty to each of them, and her life has been a constant expression of love. What I like most is the unconditionality of her love for each of them—the freedom she gives them to express their uniqueness.

One reason I am impressed with this attribute is because of what it has contributed to our family life. Our daughters' admiration for Marylyn is immense, and now that they are adults, they have formed close friendships with her. The vitality of these relationships has brought meaning to my own life. For me, it is the family in which I experience more of what matters in my living than any place else.

It was crucial for me to have a mate who shared this commitment to family, even though I didn't think much about it when we were dating. In fact, I didn't know very much about Marylyn's parenting interests or abilities when I married her. But I may have picked up more than I was aware of. I do remember how thoroughly she involved herself with my niece and nephews, and how much fun they all had together.

Is it important to you that your mate be interested in raising children? If so, you may want to observe him or her with younger sisters and brothers, nieces and nephews, or with other children. See if you are comfortable and attracted to the parenting tendencies and interaction they share.

If you desire to have a family, finding a mate who shares that goal will make your life significantly more rewarding. So make room in your mental image for the kind of partner you want when it comes to parenting.

# *Authenticity*

Some of my friends are going to accuse me of saving my favorite attribute for last. It's true that through the years I have talked more about authenticity and genuineness than any other topic. This may be because authenticity has been such a challenge for me personally. I am frequently tempted to act and react the way I think others want me to. That's what I mean by authenticity—

the ability to be completely yourself, to be forthright with your opinions and comfortable with who you are. However relevant the quest for this attribute may be in my own life, the question is the degree of importance it has for you as you build your image of the person you want to marry.

I currently have two people in marital therapy who are valiantly struggling with this issue. Lyle is the former president of a well-known American corporation. His wife, Ellen, is his equal intellectually, and she poses a dangerous threat to his sense of well-being. Here's what I mean:

Over time, Lyle has come to believe that being authentic is absolutely central for a healthy life. For many years he played the political game; he tried to satisfy everyone all the time. He let others impose their wishes on him, and he always tried to live up to everyone's expectations. But the game he played eventually damaged him. He grew tired of being phony, to the point that he wanted out of the business, even though he had become a respected and admired leader. His struggle, he now knows, was the result of not living authentically. He became successful, but at the cost of his inner peace and sense of worth.

A few years ago he began a concerted effort to be authentic and genuine, to stop worrying about what others thought of him. And he strongly encouraged his wife to do the same.

That's when the trouble started. Ellen listened to him! She started being as true to herself as she knew how to be. And "the new Ellen" clashed with Lyle. Previously docile and subservient, she didn't always agree with her husband now. She had her own ideas, opinions and perspectives. Lyle's need for total control of his environment began to collide with his desire for his wife to be emotionally healthy and authentic. He convinced her that being genuine was the most important thing in the world, but when she got good at it, he began to have doubts.

So how important is it that your mate be authentic? How free are you willing to let him or her be, especially if that freedom causes disagreements?

I'm convinced that a great marriage requires two authentic people. Don't get me wrong; many marriages survive in which one of the partners is a long way from being real and genuine. But a *great* marriage rests on the emotional stability within each of the partners. And that stability is usually the result of two people being as true to each other as they are true to themselves.

I can imagine that as you've worked your way through this chapter, you have done a lot of mental work in developing an image of your ideal marriage partner. On every one of these key points, I hope you have heard the same theme over and over again: What qualities do *you* want your mate to have? I'm convinced that a highly defined and detailed image of your ideal spouse will greatly increase the likelihood of finding that mate. The image of your "perfect person" will have a powerful influence on whom you choose to marry.

Now there is one last thing left to do. Take these 10 characteristics we have just discussed and rank them in order of their importance to you. Most of the people you consider will not be strong in each of these areas. Perhaps you'll meet someone with impeccable character, high creativity and good looks—but he or she may be lacking in ambition and spiritual depth. If you've thought through the importance of each of these qualities, and ranked them, you'll know which are essential to you and which you are willing to compromise on. Once this task is complete, I hope you'll take a little time to think about why you ranked these areas the way you did.

# THREE
# Find a Person to Love Who Is a Lot Like You

You wouldn't have to talk long with Jane and Eric to realize they are poles apart in virtually every way. She comes from a wealthy family in Cincinnati; he grew up poor on a farm in Alabama. She drives a sporty convertible; he is happy with his old clunker. She loves to party; he likes to take long walks. She likes rock music; he likes country and western. She is an extrovert; he is quiet. She likes to travel through Europe; he likes to hunt in the woods. She likes life in the fast lane; he likes it slow and simple.

How, you may ask, did these two ever get together? Well, Eric is a good-looking, six-foot-four-inch, 240-pound tight end on the university football team. He was an All-American in his sophomore year, and he has a good chance for professional stardom.

Jane is a tall and willowy cheerleader at the same school, a beautiful girl with a big smile and perfect teeth. As an active member of a prominent sorority on campus, she was encouraged to run for cheerleader at the end of her freshman year. That's where she met Eric; he was one of the judges.

They have been going together for a year and a half. Their time has been

47

punctuated by breakups and arguments. But they are a great looking couple, highly visible on their campus, and they are both terribly jealous at the thought of the other dating anyone else. Two things have held them together: They are very attracted to each other physically, and they have been extremely supportive of the other's activities.

Last month, Jane told Eric she either wanted to get engaged or call off their relationship. Eric borrowed money from his friends to buy her a ring. Soon after he proposed, they came to me for premarital counseling. I pointed out their many differences and the potential dangers, but they're still planning to get married.

So what do you think their chances are? From the little bit you know about them, how do you think they would do in a marriage?

To be completely fair, I'd have to argue that the verdict is still out. On my 50-item list (found at the end of this chapter) of important similarities, there are too many things about Eric and Jane we still don't know. For instance, are they equally intelligent? Do they have similar verbal skills and interests? Can they express their deep feelings to one another? Are they able to resolve conflicts? Are their friends and family supportive of their relationship? If the answers to these questions are all positive, it might help to balance things out.

Still, aren't you struck with how enormously difficult a marriage between these two is going to be? Do you see how hard they would have to struggle through the years just to hold their relationship together? After football and cheerleading are history, what will provide the glue for them?

## *Similarity Is Critical*

Research findings are highly consistent: *The most stable marriages are those involving two people with many similarities*.

A team of researchers administered a psychological test to three groups, each consisting of 35 couples. One group included couples who were happily married, the second group consisted of couples having trouble but planning to stay together, and the final group contained couples on the verge of separation.

The happy couples were significantly similar in general activity, friendliness and personal relations. Unhappy couples tended to be dissimilar. Both groups of unhappy couples were significantly dissimilar on emotional stability.

J. Phillippe Rushton, a professor at the University of Western Ontario in Canada, summarizes a considerable body of research:

> Several studies have shown that not only the occurrence of relationships but also their degree of happiness and stability can be predicted by the degree of matching of personal attributes. [1]

Finally, after a careful review of the literature, researchers White and Hatcher conclude:

> Clinical studies available indicate that similarity is associated with marital success and is less associated with marital instability and divorce. Evidence suggests that dissimilarity per se is associated with instability and divorce. [2]

# *Every Similarity Is an Asset*

Over the years I have become deeply convinced of this: *For couples, similarities are like money in the bank, and differences are like debts they owe.* Suppose you received two bank statements in the mail today, one showing the amount of money in your savings account, the other showing the amount you owe on your credit card. If you have a large savings account and little debt, you're in a position of strength and you can weather economic storms. If a financial crisis arises, you have the means to handle it. You can make decisions and purchases without scrambling to figure out how you'll manage.

But the reverse is also true. With big debts and little savings, you're on shaky financial ground. You have to work a lot harder to cover the bills, and you worry about job security and making ends meet.

I think you see my point. When two people come from similar backgrounds, they operate from a position of strength. Their relationship is made significantly easier by all the customs and practices they have in common. They know what to expect from each other because they have been raised by parents who were a lot alike. If these two sets of parents were similar economically, racially, religiously, politically and emotionally, their married children will enjoy a set of "agreements" that form a vital core for their union. There is incredible strength that results from this kind of commonality. It serves as a resource that can be drawn upon when problems arise. It's money in the bank!

If you want to make a marriage work with someone who is very different from you, you had better have a large number of similarities as permanent equity in your account. If you don't, your relationship could be bankrupt at a frighteningly early stage.

Why is this the case? Because every difference you have requires negotiation and adaptation. One of you has to give a lot, or both of you have to give some, and in either case there is the need for plenty of change. If couples are unwilling to bend and adjust, they'll experience regular flashes of resentment and frustration. But even if you make the necessary changes, you will still experience the kind of stress that comes whenever significant change is required. It is this stress that can threaten to destroy your relationship. If there are too many differences, you may not be able to survive all the strain involved in adapting to each other.

I know a couple, Matt and Kristen, who have a lot in common. Because their families lived only a few houses apart when they were growing up, they actually knew each other from the third grade on, and they began going together when they were juniors in high school. They were both popular in school, about equally attractive, and they had a large number of mutual friends.

Their families were both upper-middle class, active in church, and they held strong religious beliefs. While the two families had met only occasionally, they were unusually similar. There was a shared commitment to the community and especially to the activities of the three children in each family.

Matt was an athlete and Kristen wasn't, but she had as much interest in sports as he did. She read the sports page every day, knew all about the local teams, and the two of them discussed sports a lot. They listened to music, took long walks together, and talked and laughed. They were equally ambitious, similarly intelligent, liked the same shows and entertainment, both loved children, and their goals overlapped almost completely.

Following high school, they went off to college—different schools, rivals actually, but both in the same large city. They dated each other steadily, then broke off and dated others, then got back together—a pattern that continued until they were out of school. Kristen then went with her family for a year in Europe; Matt stayed home but visited her for two or three weeks at the end of her stay there. That was when they seemed to know they wanted to be together permanently. While they waited for three or four years, they were "on track" and headed in the same direction. And they were finally married nearly 10 years after their first date.

In a case like this, with so many similarities, you would think their chances of being successful in marriage would be very high. And you're right. If every couple had this much in common, the divorce rate in this country would be significantly lower. There just aren't all those differences to argue about that so many new couples have. And over the long haul, shared values and interests provide a stable environment for raising children and pursuing each partner's life goals.

Matt and Kristen were fortunate; because they came from homes with so much in common, dozens of expectations, practices and customs were the same. My list of similarities was a snap for them. They had agreement on 43 of the items going into marriage, and of the other seven, three were just a matter of some early-on negotiation. Three of the other four have never even come up.

You get my point, I'm sure. It's like these two started with a million dollars in the bank, and they owed almost nothing. They have a lifetime to enjoy their family, grow individually and build something wonderful together.

## Similarities Are Harder to Come By These Days

The divorce rate in the United States tripled between 1950 and 1980. That period saw amazing changes in this country! Just after World War II, one out of every three persons in America lived on a farm. But by 1979, only one family in 28 still lived on a farm. People were moving everywhere, leaving their extended families behind, looking for new opportunities in a country that was expanding and shifting like wildfire. Sociologists strongly agree that there was considerably less similarity between persons who married during and immediately after the second world war than those who married before it.

Obviously, all this change made finding a compatible marriage partner much more complex. If Harold Brown moved to Florida from southern Illinois and met Sally North, whose family had migrated there from New Hampshire, we have the beginnings of a partnership filled with the "need for adaptation." If Harold and Sally grew up in different parts of the country, with different customs, socio-economic backgrounds, religious upbringing and family perspectives, how could we expect them to blend smoothly and easily? That level of dissimilarity was the case for thousands of couples.

Today, people often meet and decide to marry before their two families have even been introduced. Their family roots are not intertwined at all. But only 40 years ago, which in the larger scheme of things is like yesterday, most marriages took place between two people who lived within blocks of each other and whose families had known each other for many years. Similarities abounded then; dissimilarities abound now. That's why you have to work so much harder to find the "right" mate these days.

# What Similarities Are Absolutely Essential?

Most couples are more like Harold and Sally than Matt and Kristen. So what similarities are most critical for marital happiness?

I remind you of my model: Similarities are like assets, and differences are like liabilities or debts. The total of one can best be understood in relation to the total of the other. I doubt that any single difference could sink a marriage. But there are some similarities that are incredibly strengthening to a relationship. Let me mention the ones I have found to be especially helpful.

*Intelligence.* If both individuals are similarly endowed intellectually, the marriage seems to have considerably less strain. Notice I didn't specify *education.* Some very smart people never make it to college, for one reason or another. I mean a couple needs to be in the same league intellectually. They need to see things similarly and speak about them in similar ways. If one person often feels misunderstood or senses he's being "talked down to," all kinds of emotional sparks can be triggered. Research indicates that when IQ scores are within the same general range, stability in marriage is much more likely. It doesn't matter so much *how smart* the partners are, but it does matter *how close* they are intellectually.

*Values.* We could discuss dozens of values couples need to agree on. For instance, it's a real asset when two people place a similar importance on spiritual pursuits or family life. If they don't agree, there can be intense friction between them. I always know there is going to be trouble when one person loves to go to church, Bible studies and prayer sessions, while the other has no interest in spiritual matters. This is a strong, fundamental issue that will cause clashes, perhaps frequently, as time passes.

*Intimacy.* Here I'm talking about the verbal, nonsexual variety. When both people deeply enjoy being intimate with each other and sharing their lives fully, they have an asset that will help them overcome differences throughout their lives. (We'll discuss intimacy at length in chapter 7.)

*Interests.* When there are several things two people enjoy doing together, they have a large field on which they can happily play the game of life. It is always best if these interests reach across categories. For instance, if all five of the couple's common interests are athletic, it will be less beneficial to the relationship than if the five are, for example, spread across music, sports, woodworking, theater and reading.

*Expectations about roles.* This means both partners have compatible ideas about their duties and responsibilities in the relationship and household. In this time of great change in men's and women's roles within a marriage, I have seen happy couples with a variety of viewpoints on this issue. My wife and I went to our friends' home for dinner the other night, and the man did all the cooking, serving and cleanup. His wife did very little. They seemed completely happy with one another. A number of our friends seem to be moving toward a more equal distribution of work. They appear happy, too. And some of the couples we know are very traditional—the husband is the breadwinner and she is a homemaker. The point is, if both people *agree* on the work distribution and role identification, it doesn't matter which variation they choose.

# *Differences That Spell Trouble*

If you and I had time, we could tell one story after another about couples who had some differences and still built a satisfying marriage together. I have watched people with relatively minor differences learn to adjust to one another in ways that not only held them together, but actually seemed to result in happiness for each of them.

But once we finished telling all our stories, I think we could agree that some differences are very difficult to overcome. Even though these may not result in divorce, they usually require some major changes for one or both persons, and the long-term consequences of these changes are often emotionally handicapping.

If I asked you to prepare a list of the four differences that would cause the most trouble in marriage, I wonder which ones you would name. Here is my list:

*Energy level.* When one person has a lot of energy and the other person has very little, we have the makings of major problems. This energy discrepancy may surface almost anywhere. Sometimes it shows up in the bedroom. She is eager for intimate, physical involvement three times as often as he is, while he just doesn't have the energy. Or it may become obvious in the "people" arena. He likes being involved with people—at church, after work, on the softball team—but she just wants to stay home and read a book. Sometimes it gets centered on projects around the home. She has a list of things to do around the house, but he only wants to watch television because he's tired.

*Personal habits.* When two people differ here, there can be a slow and steady erosion of their union. Here are some examples of habits that can create conflict: punctuality, cleanliness, orderliness, dependability, responsibility and weight management. We could mention dozens of other habits each person needs to consider before committing to a lifelong relationship. For instance, if one person smokes and the other doesn't, this can be a problem. If one person eats nutritional meals and the other consistently prefers junk food, that's a potential stress source.

*Use of money.* I have watched several marriages destroyed because of disagreement about finances. One person wants to save money and prepare for the future; the other wants to spend money and enjoy life to the fullest now. One wants to take risks to multiply their savings; the other wants to go at it slowly and surely. One wants to be generous with charities or with the children;

the other wants to save for themselves. Conflicting views like these can be deadly, so they must be recognized and explored before marriage.

*Verbal skills and interests.* If one person talks a lot and the other is very quiet, what can the outcome possibly be for them? If one person is just dying for more conversation, while the other is desperate for solitude and silence, there is a lot of stress! If one person talks on and on at mealtimes or on the phone, and the other person is reticent, we have all the ingredients for big trouble.

There are, of course, other potentially damaging differences we could add to this list. However, I've discovered that the four mentioned here are often the most destructive. But also beware of the relatively minor differences that can mount over time. I'm thinking about "little" things like the temperature of the room you sleep in at night, the time to go to bed and get up, the usual volume of the television or radio, the language you are comfortable using to express feelings or thoughts, the place of alcohol in the home, which television programs to watch, where you want to spend vacations, and on and on. Dissimilarities on any of these can be extremely hurtful to a relationship.

# *Qualities of Your Partner You Can't Assess*

I have encountered scores of newly married people who claimed that they knew "on their wedding night," "on their honeymoon" or "in the first month of marriage" that they had made a terrible mistake. A man wrote to me just last week:

> I can remember driving down Wabash Avenue in Chicago after the honeymoon and saying to myself, *Oh no! What have I done?* My gut told me it was a tragic decision. It took 25 years of marriage and five more years of reflection before I came to understand that I had nearly ruined my life.

Like this man, people sometimes discover they are not nearly so much alike as they thought prior to their marriage. When this happens, it is life-shattering and heartbreaking. That's why I go overboard in stressing how crucial it is to thoroughly evaluate similarities and differences before marriage.

There are some things you can't possibly know about your spouse until you're married. However, you can eliminate a lot of the risk and guesswork beforehand. An experienced psychologist or counselor can guide you through potential problem areas. I also recommend you spend hours and hours talking about the nitty-gritty aspects of life. And you may want to take some premarital tests administered by a professional. You can't be too careful.

Of course, no problem-detection system is perfect. That's why I'm going to tell you about one quality—perhaps the most important—to look for in a potential mate.

## The Personality Trait That Covers a Multitude of Differences

Over the years that I've worked as a psychologist, I've come to identify a quality in individuals that is incredibly helpful. It is called many things: flexibility, adaptability, malleability, elasticity. In essence, it makes compromise possible. Instead of cracking and falling apart when differences appear, this flexibility allows people to consider the differences, evaluate them, propose alternative solutions, and then resolve them.

It is this quality that can take over when two people discover, *after* their wedding, that they have some critical differences. If both people have a generous portion of flexibility woven into their personalities, they can make important adjustments.

My friends David and Cathy Simmonds told me recently about their honeymoon in Portugal. They had gone together for 15 months before they got married, and nearly all of that time was during David's last year in medical school and Cathy's first year of teaching. Because Cathy was engrossed with her new job and David was studying night and day, they saw each other only on weekends . . . and usually only once. They thought they knew each other fairly well, but like too many couples, they began to realize after it was too late that they had differences of all shapes and sizes.

It was in Lisbon that these differences began to surface. Cathy wanted intimacy; David wanted privacy. Cathy liked to go to bed early and get up at dawn; David was a night owl and a late sleeper. Cathy liked to eat traditional meals at traditional times; David liked to sip a little coffee in the morning, grab "whatever" in the afternoon, and then eat a big meal around eight, well after Cathy had become ravenously hungry. Cathy liked to talk a lot, just chat about anything; David talked only about the essentials. His one talk time was during dinner at night, when Cathy was tired out.

When all these differences began to pile up, they both silently feared they had made a terrible mistake. Fortunately, there were a lot of things they had in common, too, and they didn't lose sight of these. They both loved classical music, had strong religious beliefs, looked forward to having children, shared similar political positions, and they were attracted to each other physically.

As they began to recognize the kind of fix they were in, they started to think about ways to deal with it. They began to mobilize their adaptive resources. David told me, and Cathy concurred, that if they had not both grown up in large families where they had to be flexible, their marriage would not have lasted. There were many times, they said, when their differences hurt and frustrated them, when they became angry and made threats of all kinds. These times would have killed their love if they had not used their abilities to adjust.

Being flexible instead of unbending, adaptive instead of rigid, can save a couple's marriage from being destroyed by differences. Of course, it takes *two* people willing to compromise and adjust. When one partner bends and flexes every time, the relationship becomes unbalanced and "out of whack." (In chapter 8, I'll discuss how couples can learn to be flexible and adaptive.)

*Principle #3*

# *Do Opposites Attract?*

We've all known couples who could not be more different—in personality, temperament, interests, tastes and hobbies. How do these relationships usually work out?

There is a very insightful comic strip titled "Cathy," written by Cathy Guisewite. One strip shows Cathy and her boyfriend, Irving, sitting side-by-side. She is reading a book called *Love in the '90s*, while he reads the newspaper sports sections.

"According to this," Cathy says, "the thing that most attracts us to a person is the very thing that will ultimately drive us crazy, Irving."

He looks at her suspiciously.

"Fall in love with his attentiveness, and it will make you crazy that he doesn't give you enough space," she continues. "Fall in love with his drive to succeed, and it will make you crazy that all he ever thinks about is work."

Now Cathy is really into the book's message, and her left hand is high in the air with her index finger outstretched: "The quality you love most is the quality that will start to repulse you, cause your biggest fights, and rip the relationship apart!"

By this time, Irving is fed up. He has taken as much as he can take. His sports section is rolled up, and he uses it to help him make a big point: "That does it, Cathy! I am not ruining another perfectly happy Sunday morning by listening to your idiotic, self-help-book revelations!" With that, Irving walks away.

Cathy continues to read to herself: "Fall in love with her insight, and it will make you crazy that she knows too much. . . ."

The creator of this comic strip illustrates a profound point: Qualities that are attractive in the beginning of a relationship may prove difficult to live with in the long run. That's why I regularly say to people, "If the qualities that attract you to someone are different from your own, be cautious." Nearly every current psychological study indicates that it's crucial to find a spouse who is a lot like you. If they are different from you, there may be some early attraction, but the most enduring and satisfying marriages are usually ones in which the partners are very much alike.

The vast preponderance of research studies proves that you tend to be happiest with someone a lot like you. Even within our own families, we most enjoy persons who have a genetic makeup highly similar to our own.

J. Phillippe Rushton, the professor I referred to earlier, concludes, "In effect, successful human mating follows the line of genetic similarity." It's true. One of the most important principles to follow in choosing a mate revolves around a highly established reality: Stable and satisfying marriages usually involve two people who are very much alike.

# 50-Item List of Helpful Marriage Similarities

1. Socio-economic background of family
2. Intelligence
3. Formal education
4. Verbal skills
5. Expected roles for both persons within the marriage
6. Views about power distribution within the family
7. Desired number of children
8. When a family should be started
9. Child rearing views
10. Political philosophy
11. Views about smoking, alcohol and drugs
12. Amount of involvement with in-laws
13. Sense of humor
14. Punctuality
15. Dependability
16. Desire for verbal intimacy and ability to be intimate

17. The role of conflict and how to resolve it
18. The way to handle anger
19. How friendships with the opposite sex should be handled
20. Expected amount of privacy and rules for its use
21. Level of ambition
22. Life goals
23. Attitudes about weight
24. Religious and spiritual beliefs and preferences
25. Amount of church involvement
26. Family spiritual involvement
27. Hobbies and interests
28. Type of music enjoyed
29. Energy level for physical activities
30. Sexual drive and sexual interests
31. Amount of income to be spent and saved
32. How money should be allocated (clothes, vacations, etc.)
33. Amount of money to be given away and to whom
34. Degree of risks to be taken with investments
35. Attitudes about cleanliness—house, clothes, body, etc.
36. Ways of handling sickness
37. Health standards—when to see a doctor
38. Interpersonal and social skills
39. Amount and type of social involvement preferred
40. Geographical area in which to live
41. Size and style of house
42. Type of furniture and decorations
43. Amount and type of travel preferred
44. How to spend vacations
45. How to celebrate major holidays
46. How much time to spend together
47. When to go to sleep and get up
48. Temperature of home during the day and night
49. Activity during meals (talking, watching TV, etc.)
50. Television programs preferred

# FOUR
# Get Yourself Healthy Before You Get Yourself Married

A great marriage requires two healthy people, and the time to get healthy is *before* you get married. I'm not talking about nutrition and exercise, although everyone knows that physical health is important, even in marriage. Nor am I talking about spiritual health, even though I believe successful relationships are spiritually vital.

What I'm particularly concerned about here is the emotional and mental health of the two people considering a lifelong partnership. This kind of well-being contributes significantly to marital strength and happiness. In fact, when a couple is not healthy, they will inevitably damage, and maybe even destroy, their marriage.

Michelle came to me after nine years of marriage. Actually, she came only because her husband, Tom, was going to leave her if she didn't get some help. She sat in my waiting room and tried to get involved with a magazine. She was too nervous to concentrate, and she seemed relieved when I introduced myself and invited her into my office.

She was meticulously dressed. It was obvious she had anticipated this meeting for a long time and had thought carefully about what she would wear and say. She was an attractive 30-year-old woman with an easy smile and a beautiful face. But she was considerably overweight and deeply sensitive about it. Her self-consciousness seemed to contribute to a kind of shyness—a very soft voice, eyes that couldn't "fix" for very long, and a way of talking that revealed her lack of confidence.

"Tom and I were married just before my 21st birthday. He was 28 at the time," she told me. "I had worked for a year after attending junior college for four semesters. Tom didn't go to college. Actually, he didn't even finish high school. He was always smart, but he was bored, and he didn't get along very well with teachers. He was in trouble most of the time when he was in school, and he finally quit in his senior year. He went to work in his uncle's business, and he has done well. His uncle is semi-retired now, and Tom is running the business. He's quite successful, but he works long hours and isn't home very often."

I paused to see if she would continue; then I said, "Well, that's a lot of good information about Tom, but let's hear about you."

"It's easier to talk about Tom," she said slowly. "There's a lot more to him. I guess I'd say Tom swept me off my feet at a time when I didn't think much of myself. He was tall and handsome, older and wiser, and he seemed very interested in me. He took me to nice places, called me two or three times a day, and he made me feel better about myself than I had ever felt. When he introduced me to his parents, I really liked both of them. His mother immediately treated me like a daughter, and I felt like I was special to an adult for the first time. After four or five months, Tom asked me to marry him, and there was no way I could refuse."

I was beginning to understand why Michelle had called for an appointment. She had obviously been a very pretty young woman at 21, but her self-concept had never really developed. She had become involved in a romance with a man seven years older than herself, someone who had experienced problems all through school. He probably needed to buttress his own shaky self-confidence, and what better choice than someone young, beautiful and easy to control? The fact that she fit so well with his parents only increased his confidence level. So they got married.

Everything was fine for the first 18 months. Michelle continued to work, Tom did well in his uncle's business, and they bought their first little home and began to fix it up. Michelle got pregnant about then, quit her work just before their son was born and became a full-time homemaker. Tom was delighted with his son and had big dreams for him, dreams that fueled his drive to work longer hours, and he came home even more exhausted every night. He started working on Saturdays, and he was too worn out on Sundays to go to church with Michelle as they had done early in their marriage. When Michelle tried to talk about their lack of time together, Tom would apologize, promise to change and say he didn't want to hear any more about it.

Michelle began to fall apart inside. She had never been strong within herself, and the only time she felt adequate was when she was overdependent on Tom. Now her husband wasn't coming through, and she slid into depression. She would feed and take care of their little boy, and then she began to binge almost daily on all kinds of junk food. She was trying to satisfy her feelings of emptiness by putting more and more food in her stomach, but the only thing that seemed to be changing was her weight.

"Then I thought," she continued, "if we had another child, maybe I would feel better and Tom would pay more attention to me. I got pregnant, totally lost control of my weight and had our little girl. But the relief from my depression was only temporary. Two or three months after our second baby was born, Tom began to tell me how turned off he was by my body. I told him I was trying to lose weight, but actually I knew it wasn't true. That was over four years ago, and even though we love our wonderful kids, our marriage has become more and more rocky. Now I think Tom is real close to giving up. And frankly, even though I'm not sure what I would do if he left, sometimes I don't really care if he does. I don't have the slightest idea of how to get out of the hole I'm in."

# *Emotional Problems Always Do Damage*

Does Michelle's story sound familiar? There are thousands of stories essentially the same as hers. The pattern is nearly always identical, regardless of the specific emotional problems. Two people drag their emotional baggage into marriage, thinking they've found the solution to their internal trouble. In time, however, reality bursts through, and the old problems resurface, often more intensely and destructively. Soon the relationship crumbles.

In Michelle's case, she had never developed much of an identity. She didn't have many positive feelings about herself, primarily because she didn't know who she was . . . and you can't love what you don't know. She needed longer to develop, and she probably needed professional help to learn to accept and appreciate herself. She also needed wise counsel in thinking about the kind of man she should marry. Without this help, her marriage was destined for trouble.

Tom, on the other hand, had his own problems. All through school, he had never learned to manage his restless energy. Although he was bright, he was nearly always in trouble with authority figures. So he developed a set of strategies designed to keep him in control. One of those involved marrying a younger woman who was flattered by his attention and who would let him make every decision.

Like Tom and Michelle, many people think marriage will be a magical cure for their problems, that their old struggles will disappear as soon as they tie the knot. And perhaps for a while the freshness and exhilaration of their relationship hide the signs of trouble. *It's a new beginning,* the newlyweds think. *We're going to leave the old problems behind and start over.*

But inevitably, marriage only intensifies problems. The stress of marriage, the vulnerability of living with someone day in and day out, the weight of responsibility, the fear of failure, the realization that marriage isn't a cure-all—all these combine to thrust existing problems to the forefront. Michelle thought marriage would give her a "self" and magically make her feel good. In the end, she was worse off than when she started. This is the all-too-frequent consequence for couples who try to find a shortcut to resolving personal problems by getting married.

When things start getting bad, many couples "raise the ante." Instead of focusing on the root emotional problems, they begin diverting their attention by having children, pouring themselves into careers or buying expensive toys. The old problems are still there; they're just covered over. Finally, what's left is a whole family in crisis. If the individual problems had been taken care of before marriage, the entire family would have been saved a lot of pain and anguish.

## *A Biblical Case in Point*

One of the best known biblical stories involves young Jacob, who agreed to work seven years in exchange for the right to marry Laban's youngest and most beautiful daughter, Rachel.

Jacob worked hard for those seven years and fulfilled his part of the bargain. But Laban gave his *older* daughter, Leah, to Jacob!

Jacob, rightfully, was outraged, and Leah was placed in a painful position. Jacob may have liked her, but he apparently felt the kind of "like" you would have for a sister-in-law. Leah was his wife, but he *loved* Rachel.

The story turns incredibly poignant and sad. It becomes the story of a woman yearning to be loved by her husband and not knowing how to make it happen. I have frequently encountered this scenario in my practice, and the strategy Leah chose to deal with her dilemma is the same one I have heard from countless others. Listen to the rest of the 29th chapter of Genesis:

"Leah became pregnant and gave birth to a son. She named him Reuben, for she said, 'It is because the Lord has seen my misery. Surely my husband will love me now.' She conceived again, and when she gave birth to a son she said, 'Because the Lord heard that I am not loved, he gave me this one, too.' So she named him Simeon. Again she conceived, and when she gave birth to a son she said, 'Now at last my husband will become attached to me, because I have borne him three sons.' So he was named Levi. She conceived again, and when she gave birth to a son she said, 'This time I will praise the Lord.' So she named him Judah. Then she stopped having children" (Genesis 29: 32-35).

Leah's frantic search for love prompted her to have these children. The book of Genesis is full of the chaotic happenings in the lives of these sons who were conceived out of their mother's desperate attempt to be loved.

# The Foundation of Mental Health

When I want to assess clients' emotional health, I always start with their self-concept. A well-built house begins with a solid foundation. And that's what a positive self-conception is for you and me.

The self-concept is at the very center of every person's emotional and mental functioning. It is so central that any relationship between two people can be no healthier than the two "selves" involved. If you know yourself well and genuinely like yourself, you will be able to handle the daily challenges of life. But if you have a fragile sense of self, you will be susceptible to all kinds of emotional trouble. You cannot maintain healthy internal control of your life if your self-esteem is low and your self-confidence is shaky.

The critical questions in my mind are: How well constructed is this person's self-conception, and how much energy does he have for managing his inner life? If an individual seems out of touch with himself, emotionally lost or too easily upset, the seeds for emotional dysfunction have been sown. And if this individual shows disregard or disrespect—or maybe even contempt—for himself, I always expect to find many more serious problems on the "lower floors." Of course, sometimes people hide their low self-esteem by acting puffed up—boasting, denying mistakes or faults, and presenting a flawless image. Show me a person who seems overly taken with himself, overeager to get what *he* wants, and I'll show you a person with a damaged foundation.

You may be asking, "So what are some emotional problems that derive from a poorly developed self-conception, those I need to recognize in myself or in a potential mate?" Let's take a look at some.

# *Neurotics and Sociopaths*

Nearly everybody has heard the term *neurotic*, but most people don't know what it means. Don't be scared off by this psychological-sounding word. It's actually quite simple: A neurosis consists of anxiety and various behaviors designed to avoid dealing directly with the problems causing the anxiety.

Virtually every neurosis starts like this: A person feels basically inadequate at his center, so he feels threatened by ordinary, everyday problems. The response is to avoid these problems rather than face them and work through them. The defense mechanisms that are used to avoid the problems become significant problems themselves.

Many Americans suffer from some kind of neurosis, with differing degrees of severity. The form can vary a lot, but the potentially devastating effects on a marriage are enormous. If a person is regularly depressed, full of anxiety, irrationally fearful or excessively concerned about their body, they may be suffering from one of these neuroses.

Unfortunately, a neurotic often marries another neurotic, and their partnership is usually in peril from the beginning. The stresses and strains of a new marriage can make working through issues extremely complex. That's why you want to resolve problems before you get married.

As concerned as I am about the widespread existence of neuroses, I am even more concerned about sociopathic or character disorders. At the heart of these disorders is what we call "inadequate socialization." People with these disorders fail to have an effective, integrated conscience, feeling little or no guilt, remorse or anxiety. While neurotics suffer from an overactive conscience and thereby experience *too much* guilt and shame, sociopaths feel *too little*, frequently doing whatever they want with minimal concern about how their behavior may impact others.

Persons who chronically cheat and lie usually suffer from two primary deficits. First, their self-conception is not very well constructed. They don't have much ability to make good decisions, to delay gratification in their own long-term interests, and thus they are impulse-ridden—controlled by their impulses. Second, they are seriously undersocialized; that is, they have almost no regard for the rights of others. It's like the rules of living have never registered in their brains. They operate as if they are above the law, that it simply doesn't apply to them.

But they often put up an effective "front" to impress and gain the confidence of others. They usually have a smooth line. They can be downright charming, likeable, funny and entertaining. But if you let them get close to you, they will take what they want and give little in return.

It is a tragic fact that character disorders are on the increase in our society. For instance, it is estimated that there are five million Americans who have just one of these character disorders—*antisocial personality disturbance*. These people regularly violate the rights of others. They are problem children, impossible adolescents and dangerous adults. They typically lie, cheat and resist authority at every turn. They are more often male than female and usually young rather than old.

All kinds of people can have these qualities—unscrupulous businessmen, lawyers who cheat and lie, television evangelists who selfishly go after the money of older and less-advantaged persons, corrupt politicians, and, of course, drug pushers, prostitutes and others who regularly violate all the rules. Sometimes they are ordinary folks, who seem normal in every way. But behind their average-looking exterior lies a deceitful, conniving mind.

When I encounter people who cheat—and seem to have virtually no conscience about it—I know their primary relationships, especially marriage, will eventually be in trouble. They can seldom keep their problem contained, so they are not likely to be trustworthy in the intimate areas of marriage and family.

Jack had a character disorder. He constantly lied to his fiancée, Julie. He would agree to pick her up at a certain time, but he nearly always arrived 15 or 20 minutes late. More importantly, on two or three occasions, he actually took another woman out, and one time Julie found out about it. When she confronted Jack, he flat out denied it and feigned grief that Julie didn't trust him. Later, when it became clear that Jack had lied, he smoothly apologized to Julie and said he just didn't want to hurt her.

How do you spot one of these people—even if "one of these people" is you? First, you look for a lack of conscience. Do they feel any genuine guilt when they do wrong, any remorse for the hurt they have delivered? If not, they have a serious problem.

Then you look for impulsive behavior. In other words, do they have the ability to make good decisions that take into consideration your best interests—as well as their own? Or do they simply do whatever they feel like doing whenever they feel like doing it?

In addition, look for lying, cheating, taking advantage of others and placing blame on someone else for their own wrongdoing. Also, beware of big talk about high standards of morality and phony remorsefulness when they're caught in some misconduct.

When you identify these problems, don't think they'll go away or get better on their own. If you struggle with some of these problems yourself, seek professional counseling. And if your partner exhibits these behaviors, require him or her to get help. Whatever you do, don't even think about settling down with someone like this until these issues have been addressed and remedied at the deepest level.

## *Five Other Key Problems*

There are many other emotional issues that must be dealt with before a solid and successful marriage can be built. Let's look at five I frequently encounter:

• *Anger mismanagement.* The inability to handle anger effectively is the cause of countless divorces. In 1991, more than two million cases of child abuse were reported in the United States. Most experts believe there are five to 10 abuse cases for every one reported. Inability to control anger accounts for four to six million cases of spousal abuse every year. If you marry a person who is unable to control his or her anger, what chance does your marriage have? (In my book *Make Anger Your Ally*,[1] I thoroughly discuss the causes of anger and how they can be overcome.)

• *Narcissism.* This simply means an excessive admiration of oneself. For instance, I know a good-looking, 22-year-old ministerial student named Harold. He was engaged to Jamie but thought that perhaps she was "below" him, not quite on a par with him. There's nothing wrong with wondering about that, but he never once considered what kind of a partner he would be for her. He sized her up from several angles, always thinking of how she would make him look and feel. He was incredibly taken with himself, superficially in love with his wonderfulness. Although he was bright enough to mask some of his conceit and self-love, I nearly always felt unheard by him, and I sensed my opinions didn't matter to him. Harold was paying too much attention to his own needs and feelings to have any energy left to attend to me. Surely Jamie felt the same way.

The fact is that narcissism and marriage don't go together. It was Ambrose Bierce who once defined marriage as "the state or condition of a community consisting of a master, mistress, and two slaves, making in all, two." In other words, marriage partners must serve each other. Narcissists simply don't believe in taking care of anyone else. Their entire attention is focused on *their own* well-being.

• *Manic-depressive* or *cyclothymic personality disturbance.* I include this one because I've seen so many of these cases. These persons suffer, and make others suffer, from alternating periods of elation and depression. When they feel up, they are enthusiastic, ambitious, optimistic, warm and energetic. But when they feel down, they are pessimistic, negative, lethargic, critical and hard to be around. Sometimes this condition can be effectively treated with prescribed medication. Dramatic mood swings can wreak havoc in a marriage, and it's wise to see a physician *before* marriage if you suspect that you or your partner are manic-depressive.

• *Addictions.* Problems with alcohol, drugs, gambling and sex are *very* serious. If you want to walk into a marriage filled with land mines, find a spouse who has an addiction. Very few marriages survive the damaging effects of one partner's dependency.

I define an "addiction" as any behavior that negatively affects your health, work or primary relationships, and yet you continue to engage in it. Persons suffering from addictions who wish to get married will often make claims to bypass the necessary treatment. For instance, they will repeatedly and vehemently deny having a problem. Or they will insist they can stop doing it voluntarily, whenever they want. This is almost never the case.

For the person contemplating marriage, it's often difficult to detect an addiction. Like sociopaths, addicts are extremely skilled at covering up and hiding their problem. You may think, *Certainly I could tell if someone drinks too much or takes drugs.* But often you can't. If you even remotely suspect this type of problem with your spouse-to-be, I suggest you read books on the subject and talk to a professional counselor about the telltale signs of addiction.

If you are the one who has a problem like this, I strongly encourage you to seek professional help or to get involved in a 12-step program as soon as possible. The same strong advice applies to your partner if he or she is the one who is addicted.

• *Parental issues.* Under ordinary circumstances, our mothers and fathers are the most important developmental influences in our lives. We learn thousands of things from them during our growing-up years and even later. Some of these things we learn by observing them; other learnings emerge from their verbal instruction and advice. But by far the most important learning we receive from our parents comes from our relationship with them,

73

which begins almost from conception and certainly from the point of birth. In this relationship with each of our parents we learn to trust people or fear them, to be adventurous or stay carefully within safe limits, to be intimate with others or remain distant, to think and feel freely or protect ourselves with internal defenses. In our relationships with our parents there will be times of close identification with them, and sometimes we may be confused about who we are and who they are.

Harville Hendrix has a very helpful section in his best-selling book *Getting The Love You Want*:

> A child's success at feeling both distinct from and connected to its mother has a profound impact on all later relationships. If the child is fortunate, he will be able to make clear distinctions between himself and other people but still feel connected to them; he will have fluid boundaries that he can open or close at will. A child who has painful experiences early in life will either feel cut off from those around him or will attempt to fuse with them, not knowing where he leaves off and others begin. This lack of firm boundaries will be a recurring problem in marriage.[2]

It is imperative that before entering marriage, you work through and clarify these parental relationships. If you don't, you'll inevitably transfer negative and incomplete learnings to the new "primary person" in your life.

When we marry, it will be ideal if in relation to our parents (1) we are essentially free from them—emotionally independent individuals—so we do not have to make decisions and live our lives to please them; (2) we are clear about what is particularly true of our relationship with our mother and father, and what is true in relation to our spouse. When we confuse these relationships, we leave our spouse feeling violated and helpless; and (3) we have established a relationship with our parents in which they will not intrude in our marriage, will not dictate to us in any authoritative ways, and yet we can still maintain a closeness and connectedness to them.

When this ideal is not realized before marriage, there may be problems in the new relationship. I can think of hundreds of potential conflicts, but consider the three that are most related to the points just presented: (1) Some people will feel a need to run home or be on the phone with Mom or Dad frequently to ask advice. Or they will always worry that they must make decisions in just the way Dad or Mom want them to. This leaves their mate feeling like he or she has married a committee rather than an individual; (2) One person will relate to a mate exactly as he's learned to relate to his parent of the opposite sex. So the partner always feels that the responses and behavior he or she receives is intended for someone else; and (3) The parents step beyond reasonable boundaries—"Dad says we must not buy the house" or "Mom says we need to work at Grandma's house on Saturday." When parents are intrusive, marriages suffer intensely.

## So What Does It Mean to Be Emotionally Healthy?

We've looked at what it means to be unhealthy; now what about the other side of the coin? What does it mean to be emotionally healthy?

I was thinking about that the other day as I was eating lunch in my office with my close friend Dr. Lewis Smedes. I told him I had been puzzling over why I like him so much. He didn't interrupt me to say he was bored or embarrassed, so I just thought out loud for a little while.

"What I like so much about you, Lew," I said, "is that I trust you at a deep level. What I trust about you is your ability to be authentically yourself—and thereby to be faithful to you, to me and to the truth."

In his characteristic way, he stuttered just a bit and said, "How exactly do you mean that?"

"Well," I replied, "it seems as if you feel so secure inside that you can listen to all the sides on any issue, weigh the information, and then stand in the middle of all that and come to your own conclusion. Your position always seems so wise, so free of initial prejudice, so responsive to the facts. And then you are able to tell me where you stand without making me feel that I'm wrong—even if you disagree with me."

It was in that conversation that I began to get a better hold on the fundamental elements involved in being healthy.

First, there is a kind of *inner security* in healthy people. They are not always thinking that their worth as a person is on the line, that they have to be "right" in order to be acceptable and valuable. I think this kind of security comes from good parenting in which unconditional love is given and received at a deep level. When you get loved like this, an inner security naturally develops.

I also think a healthy person has an enormous *respect for the truth*. We know that the truth is always based on eternal values and absolutes. It is the guiding force behind all of your decisions—from big matters, like who you will marry, to little matters, like which TV program you will watch right now. The truth may be hard to discern sometimes, but the healthy person tries to get as close to it as possible, because he knows truth will contribute to deeper meaning, better relationships and a more satisfying life.

Healthy people also know that the way to the truth involves *collecting all the information*, allowing all the data to be known. This is why they listen so carefully and want to know what you really think. They don't worry about whether your opinion is different from their own. Their security isn't threatened by being different.

Then they *weigh the information* they have collected. They place "values" on different parts of the information through the use of careful, although usually unconscious, internal processes that are deeply influenced by well-established moral codes, a value system that informs all decision making.

Finally, healthy people are *authentic*—that is, they stand in the middle of all the information they have collected, and they come to a decision or a position that is the closest approximation to the truth. With courage and total commitment, they state that position as honestly as they know how—and they live in accordance with it until they change in light of some new information. Still, they aren't arrogant, assuming their position and the truth are exactly the same. They don't make you feel you are wrong if you disagree with them. They have a deep humility that seems to emanate from their recognition that they are very fallible, that while they need to come to the best position possible, they also recognize your right to do the same.

That's the kind of healthy person I have found Lew Smedes to be, and I think it's the kind of person you and I want to be. If you can get yourself healthy like this before you get yourself married, what an enormous contribution you will make to your mate and to your marriage.

## How Can You Become Healthy If You're Not Healthy Now?

A lot of studies have indicated that the healthiest marriages involve two people who have experienced healthy childhoods. If we get a good combination of deep love and careful instruction from nurturing parents, we will inevitably become healthy ourselves.

But what happens if our parents were anything but healthy? How can we unlearn all the unhealthy ways we picked up from them? Let me make four suggestions about becoming healthy:

• *Find a source that offers unconditional love, the kind of love you needed when you were a child.* Admittedly, good sources for this kind of love are hard to come by. Maybe you can find one in a close friend or relative. I try to be a good source as a psychotherapist, and most therapists try to do the same. Healthy churches offer unconditional love, and I have personally found the best source of love to be the love of God. Wherever you find this kind of love, it is worth everything you have.

• *Learn to love yourself.* It isn't enough that someone else loves you, even if that someone is God. You have to accept the fact that you *are* lovable. When you do, you'll discover you don't have to fabricate a self in order to please someone else and earn their love. You can just be the authentic you.

• *Find someone who will regularly encourage, inspire, listen to and challenge you.* I have some close friends who do this for me. We all need close friends, because it's hard—maybe impossible—for us to understand our emotions and know exactly what we're feeling and thinking deep within ourselves. We need someone to help us sort through our thoughts and feelings, and help us confront our problems.

• *Cultivate relationships with people who will help you take a stand, be authentic and feel secure in your positions.* We all need people who will stay with us, cheer us on, bolster our shaky confidence and reinforce our courage. An ongoing support system helps us stay on track, even when we feel like falling back into unhealthy patterns.

This is what it takes to get ourselves healthy. We need to be "reparented" in a kind, loving and thoughtful way by genuinely healthy people. Often these persons are friends or family members, but sometimes people need the assistance and guidance of a well-trained and caring psychotherapist.

However you go about it, and whomever you find to help you, the important thing is to get yourself emotionally healthy prior to marriage. The healthier you are, the healthier your marriage will be.

# FIVE
# Find a Love
# You Can Feel Deep in Your
# Heart—and Express
# It Carefully

My favorite comic strip is Calvin and Hobbes, written by a genius named Bill Watterson. It is by far the most insightful and delightfully funny comic strip I've ever read. It features a little boy named Calvin and his stuffed tiger, Hobbes, who is alive for Calvin but no one else.

One day the two are out walking in the snow, and Calvin asks Hobbes, "What's it like to fall in love?"

Hobbes stops walking, looks into space and strokes his chin. "Well, say the object of your affection walks by . . ."

"Yeah?" says Calvin, looking up at his friend expectantly.

"First, your heart falls into your stomach and splashes your innards," Hobbes says, swinging his hand around to demonstrate. "All the moisture makes you sweat profusely." He wipes his forehead. "This condensation shorts the circuits to your brain, and you get all woozy. When your brain burns out altogether, your mouth disengages and you babble like a Cretin until she leaves."

"*That's* love?!" Calvin asks, obviously shocked.

"Medically speaking," Hobbes intones, clearly very taken with his own description.

Calvin concludes: "Heck, that happened to *me* once, but I figured it was *cooties!*"

Hobbes' creator, Bill Watterson, may not be considered an international expert on the subject of love, but there's some illuminating insight here, don't you agree? When he speaks "medically" about the nature of love, Hobbes comes amazingly close to describing that set of wild internal happenings that accompany love. I know what it is to have my brain short out, to feel woozy and know my mouth is babbling without *any* direction from my burned-out control center. It's an ecstatic, high feeling. I hope you've had this powerful experience, too.

Someone once said, "Love is only for the young, the middle-aged, and the old." For everyone, love is a powerful force that energizes our lives and revolutionizes our relationships. Love can transform momentary struggles into compelling adventures. It can magically change hard work into wonderful opportunities. It can motivate courageous behavior. Love is the greatest thing in the world, and when two people feel it forcefully, it deserves their deepest respect and appreciation. As writer Pierre Teilhard de Chardin said, "Someday after we have mastered the air, the winds, the tides, and gravity, we will harness for God the energies of love. And then for the second time in the history of the world, man will have discovered fire."

When two people are in love, they want to be with each other all the time. There is a total involvement with the other. When they are together, their biochemistry may activate a "floating" sensation. And when they are separated, they can't wait to be together again. All of this togetherness is designed to introduce them to each other—on one deep level after another.

During this blissful happiness and contentment, there aren't enough words to say how they feel. I am reminded of Judith Viorst's comment:

> Brevity may be the soul of wit but not when someone's saying "I love you." When someone's saying "I love you," he always ought to

give a lot of details: like, why does he love you? and, how much does he love you? And, when and where did he first begin to love you? Favorable comparisons with all other women he ever loved are welcome, and even though he insists it would take forever to count the ways in which he loves you, you wouldn't want to discourage him from counting.[1]

# The Purpose Behind the Passion

I doubt medical science or psychological research could ever fully explain why two people are drawn together. But I have a theory: I believe initial attraction is a kind of match between a real person and a "dreamed-about person." For many years, you've formulated a vision of your ideal mate. Then suddenly, you meet someone who comes close to fulfilling this vision, triggering a powerful internal release of chemicals that results in the kind of experience Hobbes describes so well. Part of this "dream" involves physical characteristics—body shape, facial appearance, smell, skin texture and hair color. Sometimes this "match" occurs on the basis of appearance alone, but for other people, it becomes obvious only when they touch or kiss.

I'm sure you've read or seen Shakespeare's famous play *Romeo and Juliet*. When Romeo caught sight of Juliet across a crowded room, something like love at first sight exploded within him. When they spoke, Juliet felt the same wild emotions. Even though their families were sworn enemies, the two young lovers were hopelessly taken with each other. Maybe you've experienced similar emotions.

As wild and passionate as these feelings are, they usually don't last very long—at least in this form and to this degree. Like Hobbes intimates, our whole insides would be "laid to waste" if they did. However, passionate love performs a powerful service as long as it lasts. It focuses the total attention of two people on each other long enough for them to build an enduring structure for their relationship. The passionate love experience will never hold the two of them together forever. But building "enduring structures" for a relationship takes a lot of time and effort, and if two people are not attracted to one another physically, the hard work might never get done.

I suspect that at least part of the internal process that makes your "heart fall into your stomach" is the powerful realization that you've found a person who can satisfy your deepest needs and desires. We all have many needs—physical, sexual, social and relational. But the most powerful ones have to do with our sense of self. We vitally need to know that another person finds us desirable, attractive and lovable. And if this other person is someone we value and admire, the idea that he or she feels this way about us is overwhelming. To be found attractive just the way we are—without any apparent need for change—is a powerful experience.

That's another function of passionate love—the life-changing experience of being accepted and valued. When two people find themselves totally engrossed in each other, they often experience a dramatic boost in their self-esteem. For in the process of discovering that someone else finds them attractive, they begin to see themselves as attractive, too. Passionate love focuses a bright, positive light on each of the persons involved, and both of them fall in love not only with each other but also with themselves.

Psychologists Ellen Berscheid and Elaine Walster have concluded that attraction occurs when we believe that others (1) like us; (2) have highly similar views to our own on political, social, economic and religious issues; and (3) are eager to support us if we are lonely, fearful or under stress.[2] In fact, empirical research indicates that our selection of a mate is designed to bolster our own self-esteem. When we experience a strong surge of emotion for someone, certainly part of the reason is because we feel so validated. We love this person partially because he or she makes us feel good about ourselves.

The fact is that love is a powerful therapeutic agent in *every* relationship. Dr. Karl Menninger, one of America's most outstanding psychiatrists, held that "love cures people—both the ones who give it and the ones who receive it."

If someone we respect and value feels good about us, our most pressing emotional quest will be satisfied. It often takes this kind of experience with a person of the opposite sex to convince us that we *are* lovable, and that it is legitimate to feel good about who we are.

# *Evaluating "Like" Versus "Love"*

Sometimes a man and a woman have a lot in common and seem "right" for each other in many ways—but there is no chemistry, no magic, nothing that resembles passionate love. They may be trusted friends, filled with respect and admiration for each other., but their relationship seems more like a brother and sister. Could this develop into marriage?

First, let me say that many marriages begin as friendships. Regardless of what poets and songwriters say about love at first sight, the fact is that some couples feel no exhilarating, romantic feelings early in their relationship. Sometimes the strong emotions absent in the beginning gradually grow as the relationship deepens. Just because friends don't feel passionate love initially doesn't mean the relationship should be permanently written off. At the very least they have a great friendship, and it *may* develop into a lot more over time.

The problem comes when people try to force a friendship into a romance. A strong friendship can be a foundation for a marriage, but when there's no natural attraction or emotional sparks, a deeper relationship can't be forced. One of my longtime psychology colleagues, Dr. Paul Roberts, believes that two people must experience genuine attraction to one another before they should consider a deeper relationship. He has worked with married couples for many years, and he has found it difficult to build successful marriages when one or both partners feel little physical attraction to the other. Dr. Roberts believes that the desire to touch, hold hands and hug is critical for long-term satisfaction. I agree. Building a great marriage is virtually impossible without the attraction and excitement that come with passionate love.

# Passionate Love Can Make or Break a Relationship

I think God's invention of passionate love is one of the most magnificent parts of His creation. I am convinced that every person should have the opportunity to enjoy this kind of love at some time. There is no substitute for the deep-down love that two people have for one another. But in the early phases of a relationship, great care must be given to the expression of these feelings. Passionate love has a way of shorting out the brain and squashing rational thought. If conscious control is not exerted, the euphoric couple will begin to behave in ways that are damaging to the relationship and each individual.

This inevitably brings up the question, "How far should you go sexually prior to marriage?" This is not a book about sexuality, but that's an important question in regard to mate selection. (For a thorough discussion of this topic, I recommend the excellent book *The Gift of Sex* by Clifford and Joyce Penner.)

I am deeply convinced that any two people who choose to marry need to maintain clear minds until the moment they say "I do." Because of this, I believe in sexual abstinence prior to marriage. Sexual intercourse before marriage is a clear act of commitment! Once you have become sexually involved with a potential mate, your ability to think clearly and objectively becomes impossible.

That's one reason premarital intercourse is destructive. In one impulsive moment, two people cut short the process of "choosing" one another, and they rob themselves of their own wisdom. Once they are sexually involved, they forfeit their combined ability to make a wise, unhindered decision. Countless couples are swept away by the powerful feelings that accompany sex, and their head-in-clouds mind-set leads them to marriage. In time, however, the intense emotions may fade, and they may discover many problems and differences in their relationship.

Just a few decades ago, our society discouraged sex prior to and outside of marriage. Cultural values were such that persons had a strong sense of right and wrong, and they followed (or tried to at least) the larger moral code. Things have changed! TV, movies, commercials, magazines, billboards, radio shows—everything encourages a permissive, anything-goes attitude. This systematic attack on traditional values has contributed significantly to poor mate selection and resulting marital failure in the United States. In my opinion, the fragmentation of marriages and families is more than a little the result of trivializing sexual expression.

We have consistently conveyed a message to singles that sexual behavior is inevitable—even acceptable—apart from the development of other aspects of the relationship. In this society we have winked at full sexual activity outside of marriage, and in so doing we have set ourselves up for significant damage in the area of family formation and, ultimately, societal stability.

Lest you consider me a prude, let me assure you I am quite aware of what goes on. As a psychologist, I am daily ushered into the most intimate chambers of people's lives. I know how they think, feel and behave. On this subject, I consider myself a realist; I know how people are relating sexually. I also know the results of this behavior.

The longer I listen to people's most intimate stories, the more I know that there must be a revolution in our thinking about sexual expression. If we want to have strong families that emerge from wise selections of marriage partners, we need to overhaul our reasoning about the relationship between love and sex. If we continue telling single persons that sexual intimacy is healthy at whatever stage of their relationship, they will continue getting married for all the wrong reasons. Once they have made this fundamental error, their marriage—and ultimately their family—will evolve into a struggle with no winners. After all, everyone loses when a marriage breaks apart—wounded spouses, victimized children, extended family and even friends.

Even as I write this, the cover story of *People* magazine features the marriage of two well-known celebrities, John Tesh and Connie Sellecca. They dated for one year and chose premarital abstinence on the basis of their beliefs and values. The novelty of their choice was so shocking to the writer of the article that "premarital abstinence" was the focus of the story.

There is good news, however. I'm convinced we are going to see a return to this value across our nation. Radical sexual permissiveness has done terrible damage to the most intimate part of our nation's nurturing system. For too long, the mate-selection task has been seriously compromised, and the pain we have experienced because of ill-advised pairings will drive us back to traditional values. As a society, we will again make sexual involvement a celebration and symbol of lifetime marital commitment.

# *Principles for Expressing Passionate Love*

One of the most mature couples I have ever seen for premarital counseling came to me last year. Sandy was in her first year of teaching, while Peter was finishing his last semester of college. They had met four and a half years earlier and had dated seriously for nearly three years by the time I met them. They were working through two or three difficult issues, and their long-term future as a couple was very much in question.

Peter and Sandy were well matched, with a solid relationship. They certainly were attracted to each other physically. In fact, that was one reason they came to see me. They were becoming more and more physically involved, and they knew it was biasing their decision about whether they should marry each another.

Complicating factors involved their differing backgrounds. Peter came from a home in which traditional values about sex had been taught with unusual candor and thoroughness. His parents had talked with Peter and his older brother on many occasions about sexuality—explaining, discussing, answering questions and sharing value perspectives. Out of all this came Peter's desire to wait until marriage to have intercourse. This desire had strong roots in his Christian faith, but it also made sense to him from a psychological standpoint. He knew how distorted his perspective became when his physical involvement got ahead of his emotions and intellect.

Sandy's upbringing was quite different. Her parents were divorced when she was very young. She barely knew her father, and her mother never discussed sexuality. What's worse, Sandy's mother was flirtatious and sexual with the men she dated. Even as a child, Sandy thought her mother's behavior was inappropriate. Obviously, Sandy didn't have the moral training that Peter had. But in high school she got involved with Young Life, a "club" for high school students. Here, she heard teaching on sexuality and had numerous opportunities to talk with peers and adults.

Now, years later, Peter and Sandy were struggling to keep their sexual desires in control. They knew if they went too far, their decision about marriage would be compromised. They experienced powerful feelings for each other, but what they wanted most was to make a wise determination about their future together. They were confused and struggling when they asked for my help.

Here are the five points I worked on with Peter and Sandy, and I believe these principles apply to everyone:

**1.** Passionate love between two people is a crucial ingredient if they are to have a long and satisfying relationship. Some psychologists, counselors and authors disregard the importance of romantic feelings and physical attraction. I suppose they are concerned about the dangers of relying too heavily on emotions and the problems resulting from decisions made in the heat of the moment. It's true that emotions can be misleading, and physical attraction is just one part of the mate-selection process. However, I maintain that passionate love is absolutely *vital* to any enduring relationship.

**2**. Passionate love always involves strong physical attraction. If a couple experiences genuine love for each other, they will find themselves wanting to hold and kiss each other, and express themselves sexually. These desires follow directly and naturally from their love for each other. They are a fundamental part of everyone's biological and psychological makeup. In fact, if you don't feel your partner's strong physical desire to be close to you, something may be missing. A lack of affection or desire for physical intimacy should raise a red flag in your mind.

**3**. Physical involvement must be managed with extreme care. Strongly defined boundaries need to be agreed upon, and there has to be self-discipline exerted to stay within those limits. Otherwise, sexual expression can take control of the relationship and blind the couple to reality. I have encountered scores of couples who failed to keep their emotional development and commitment coordinated with their physical involvement. One couple after another has told me they made a decision about marriage because they were so physically involved. In fact, some married couples have told me their marriage became a "foregone conclusion" because they were so involved sexually. All other considerations about their relationship were "covered over" because of their out-of-control passion.

Of course, balance is critical here. Couples need not stifle their feelings completely. I have seen married couples in therapy who never recaptured the passionate love for one another they denied and pushed away while dating. It is far better to work on managing behavior through carefully chosen limits.

**4**. Every progression of physical activity establishes a new plateau—and it is extremely difficult to retreat once it has been reached. Each level of sexual experience is so immediately rewarding that it's nearly impossible to be satisfied by previous levels. That's why every new step of sexual expression must be carefully chosen by both people. This may sound rigid to many because it runs counter to the popular thinking in our society. But if sexual expression is allowed complete freedom, and if spontaneity is treated as a primary virtue, this expression will simply develop "a mind of its own," without any concern for long-term consequences. I cannot overstate how much damage this kind of "free and spontaneous" expression has wrought in the mate-selection process.

**5**. When sexual expression is not kept in check, the emotional, cognitive and spiritual aspects of the relationship become slaves to the physical desires. Let me say it again: Physical attraction is critical, but it needs to develop in a coordinated way with other parts of the relationship.

Love, then, is a highly complex process about which we know far too little. What we do know is that without it, there are no great marriages. When it is present for two people, however, their relationship is the most vital part of their lives. It contributes energy and focus to their partnership.

Unfortunately, passionate love between two people does not necessarily indicate that their life together will be fulfilling and harmonious. The decision about marriage involves many other considerations. In order to make a good decision, two people must often enjoy their love for each other at the same time they struggle against letting it become dominant in their efforts to make a solid choice.

This becomes one of the most difficult parts of the mate-selection process. A woman and a man must experience and enjoy passionate love for each other, but they must maintain their objectivity about the most important relational decision they will ever make. It is a herculean challenge that is at once deeply satisfying and highly demanding. Love is experienced in the heart, but the decision about marriage is carefully protected until the moment that permanent commitment is pledged. If both of these goals are reached, love can flourish in a marriage that will last a lifetime.

# SIX
# Let Passionate Love Mature Before You Decide to Marry

Susan Jordan had never known anyone quite like Darrin, and she certainly hadn't *dated* anyone like him. He was sensitive and caring, fun and spontaneous, responsible and hard working. Susan was very attracted to him physically, and all the people close to her were tremendously impressed with him. Equally important, he thought she was wonderful!

For the first two months of their relationship, he had called her several times a day, and he wanted to see her whenever their schedules would allow. He took her to nice places, bought her presents and said all the right things.

Everything was great—almost. Susan had a nagging fear that grew worse as the weeks passed. She knew Darrin had broken off two other relationships when the early excitement started leveling off. Apparently, he figured he wasn't really in love if the passion and ecstasy of newborn romance began to fade.

Susan knew that Darrin's previous girlfriends had been confused and shattered when Darrin ended their relationships without warning or logical explanation. Susan didn't want this to happen to her. But she sensed that Darrin was growing restless, and she desperately wanted to break his pattern.

I worked with Susan on the problem of transitioning from "passionate love" to what is sometimes called "companionate love." Professor Bernard Murstein describes this latter kind of love this way:

> Companionate love . . . may be defined as a strong bond including tender attachment, enjoyment of the other's company, and friendship. It is not characterized by wild passion and constant excitement, although these feelings may be experienced from time to time. The main difference between passionate and companionate love is that the former thrives on deprivation, frustration, a high arousal level, and absence. The latter thrives on contact and requires time to develop and mature.[1]

Murstein's companionate love is what long-term, committed relationships are made of. It is a far deeper kind of love than the fiery, hot-blooded emotions that characterize early romance. Companionate love involves communication, commitment, caring, affection and support for one another. There are shared experiences and times of unhurried relating that are less frequently charged with physical excitement and high-flying emotions.

The transition from passion to tender attachment is absolutely critical, but it doesn't always happen. As a matter of fact, I am convinced that companionate love never develops in 75 percent of the cases, even when passionate love offers initial promise. That's why no decision about the permanency of a relationship should ever be made until a couple has given this sturdier kind of long-lasting love a chance to grow.

As for Darrin and Susan, fading passion didn't have the last word. Susan's brilliant reading of Darrin's "love" pattern got her to my office in time. Actually, Susan got *Darrin* to my office in time. We worked for three months on his misreading of his own reality. He came to recognize that staying in love doesn't require constant passion. This freed him to pursue companionate love. He and Susan built a lasting relationship with steel-reinforced companionate love all through the structure.

# *Why Most Relationships Don't Survive When Passion Fades*

When passionate feelings are running high, lovers think their relationship will last forever. *I feel so wonderful,* the partners may think. *This is it! This is the love I've been looking for!* But inevitably the fever pitch cools off, and a seed of doubt is sown. What then? If the couple can develop companionate love, they stand a good chance of staying together. However, my experience has shown that frequently one or both persons will not stick around when passion fades. There are four primary reasons why most relationships never get beyond the stage of passion or infatuation:

1. Some people are addicted to all the excitement that is present in the early phases of the "passion period." Can you imagine any drug-altered state more intense than the one Hobbes described to Calvin in the last chapter? When "your heart falls into your stomach and splashes your innards" and "when the condensation shorts the circuits to your brain and you get all woozy," it is an experience seldom equaled. Like a drug addict constantly in search of his next high, some people simply thrive on supercharged feelings. So they date one person after another, relishing the thrill of soaring emotions—as long as they last. Others go ahead and get married, only to find that the passion abates, sometimes disappearing for long stretches of time. Then they seek the "turn-on" experience in extramarital encounters, pornography, or in some other way. The fact is, these people are *addicted* to "passion surges," and they need help to get free of their imprisonment.

2. Some people simply don't want to move on to the next stage. They know that companionate love is well on the road to marriage, and they are deeply frightened of commitment. There are many reasons for this fear, some perfectly understandable and others indicative of deeper problems. A lot of these people know how much it takes to make a marriage work, and they don't consider themselves ready. Some of them have grown up with divorced

parents, and they're afraid of replicating that pain. A few of them fear the responsibilities of maturity. Whatever the case, they put on the brakes just when passion could begin transitioning into something much deeper, and they refuse to let the relationship proceed.

3. Some people simply don't know how to move to the next stage. They've never done it before, and the challenge is beyond them. It means getting to know themselves and another person at a deep level, and working through the tangles they will inevitably experience. They've got the dating scene down pat—where to go, how to make small talk, when to call for the next date. But they are unpracticed in the process of inner exploration, self-revealing and careful listening. They need help learning to merge their own life with someone else's.

4. Sometimes passionate love fails to develop into a deeper love because one or both people recognize their relationship is just not right. It's simply not sturdy enough to make it through the inevitable problems of married life. And when this happens, the dating process has worked. The final verdict is "Don't get married." Even though this may bring sadness, think of the alternative. Someone has said that the best divorce is the one that happens *before* two people get married.

So this final reason passionate love never develops into companionate love is because two people are not right for each other. They don't belong together, and if they tried to force it, they would end up battered and beaten. Maybe you wonder why their passionate love worked so well, why they got so "fired up" about each other. My theory is that passionate love relates to more primitive parts of ourselves—our biological parts that are basically blind to countless relational factors. Companionate love involves deeper and more personal aspects. It is not at all uncommon for two people to find that after their romance and passion have leveled off, there is not enough depth to their relationship to make it permanent. At this point, the only reasonable course is to break up. It's usually painful, but it's always an important discovery. Thank God when the discovery comes *before* marriage.

# *Some Couples Stay Together But Go Nowhere*

Sometimes realizing a relationship is not "a match made in heaven" is especially painful for one or both of the persons. So a conspiracy develops to hide the truth. I have known couples who kept going together long after they inwardly acknowledged that their relationship had no chance of becoming permanent. Nobody likes to hurt another person, so some people perpetuate the charade, rather than face the truth. They continue limping along together because they have a friendship with each other, however superficial it may be. Separating would mean an abrupt re-entry into the old world of lonely weekends and the old fear that "the right one" might *never* come along.

In this situation, the decision to separate has been made, but it's too emotionally demanding for the couple to admit it to themselves and to each other. I suppose there's nothing wrong with their staying together for a while to work through the fears, disappointments and heartaches of a breakup. But it becomes destructive if they get stuck in this spot and feel imprisoned because they have not been honest with each other.

Connie and Jim were caught in this trap. Both had been married before; Jim for 15 years, producing four children, and Connie for two years, with no children. Connie sold advertising for a national magazine, and she was remarkably successful, earning more than twice as much as Jim. He worked as the manager of a sporting goods department in a large downtown store. Connie had a master's degree; Jim had taken only a few courses in junior college. But their differences were more central. Connie had worked hard on her inner life; she knew herself well at a deep level. Jim had no interest in "all that emotional stuff." He willingly listened to Connie talk about her deep feelings and thoughts, but he had none of his own to share. He was spiritually and emotionally frozen, like a walking iceberg, and Connie felt frustrated and alone when she tried to get below the surface with him.

The two of them continued to date for months after Connie had determined there was no future for them. Why would she perpetuate a relationship she knew was going nowhere? When I asked her that question, she said it was for three reasons: (1) They were very attracted to one another. The chemistry in their relationship had always been strong, and the passionate emotions were so exhilarating that Connie didn't want to give them up; (2) Before Jim came into her life, Connie experienced terrible loneliness. Without Jim, she feared, the weekends would be just as empty as they were in the past; (3) Connie dreaded giving Jim the bad news. She had never led him on by talking about their future together, and she had even discussed her frustrations on several occasions. But the thought of telling him that they were through was almost more than Connie could handle. So their relationship dragged on. Passionate love never developed into companionate love, and the relationship died a long, slow death.

There are countless reasons why people perpetuate a dead-end relationship. These usually revolve around fear: Fear that they may not find anyone else, or anyone as good or better; fear that they may be walking away from a relationship that might work if only they tried harder; or fear that they might do irreparable damage to the other person—damage they would regret for a lifetime. All of this fear combines to keep them frozen. They are not happy, nor very hopeful. Yet they lack the courage to leave.

Some people finally get married to a person about whom they have serious misgivings. However, too many failed marriages involve fantasy triumphing over fact. People wish the relationship could work, and their imagination takes over. They keep imagining, and wishing, and they remain in the relationship far too long. Sometimes they stay so long that they feel ashamed to leave. Eventually they go against their best judgment and commit themselves to a person for whom their love is superficial and inadequate.

I encourage these persons to seek professional counseling *before* they get married—to gather their courage and face the facts. Once they marry, their choice vanishes. The goal then is to make the marriage work. Whatever the misgivings, marriage changes the focus from consideration to commitment.

# *What Does Companionate Love Look Like?*

I have talked with scores of couples—some married and some un-married—and I think I know what companionate love looks like. I have watched it in its earliest form when it begins to bud between two people. I have observed it take shape in relationships during the exciting middle phases. And I have studied it and admired it during the peak of its expression. Let me briefly share with you seven observations I have made about companionate love.

• *Enduring love involves an unselfish commitment to your lover's happiness.* Harry Stack Sullivan was a brilliant psychiatrist, and his writings were very influential when I was in graduate school. He once said, "Love begins when a person finds another person's needs to be as important as his own." When you begin to sense that the person you love is becoming more and more aware of the "real you" and trying to help you get your deepest needs satisfied, you are on the edge of a rich and fulfilling experience. Likewise, when you find that your lover's needs and desires are as important to you as your own, genuine love is being born. When that realization dawns upon you, you will be experiencing the kind of love that can sustain a long-term relationship.

• *Companionate love compels you to enjoy what your partner enjoys.* Let me share an example from my own marriage. I love baseball. I'm a tireless Chicago Cubs fan, and I have been all my life. If you're a Cubs fan, you have to be tireless—the last time they won the World Series was in 1908. If you're the spouse of a Cubs fan, there are many reactions you could have, especially if you have to live with the daily telecasts of the games. My wife must have decided long ago that my love for the Cubs was never going to wane, however hard they might try to discourage it. So out of her love for me, Marylyn became a secret Cubs fan herself. She would give almost anything for them to win the World Series or the National League pennant—or just give a good showing. She wants me to be happy, so she quietly pulls for the Cubs. You might say she even "loves" the Cubs, but I'm smart enough to know that who she really loves is me. The Cubs for her are lovable only because she cares deeply for me.

I used to puzzle over the fact that some couples seem to have so many interests in common, while others have so few. In time, however, I have discovered that very few share these interests *naturally*. Rather, they are *developed*. They love each other so much that they start enjoying what their lover enjoys.

• *People who love each other deeply recognize the value of developing three spaces in their relationship—one for him, one for her, and one for them.* This may seem contradictory to my last point, but it really isn't. Common interests are important, but equally important are individual interests. I have a sister and brother-in-law who have mastered this secret of loving. While they do a lot together, they also have time apart. Ferne is a singer and longtime member of Sweet Adelines, the international singing group. She travels all over the country to sing and judge and socialize with her many friends. Her husband, Dick, a psychologist who first attracted my interest to the field, has always supported Ferne's singing, but he is a fisherman. He frequently joins a group of friends for a week of lake fishing. The separate hobbies for these two provide opportunities to gain experiences and refresh themselves. When they come together, they have more to offer each other.

• *People who love each other in a mature and enduring way seem to recognize the importance of finding individual wholeness, and they know this usually comes during periods of quietness and solitude.* These couples know that deep down in their individual center lie the richest mine fields of meaning. Successfully cultivating inner thought and feeling requires an elimination of the static that is so much a part of our everyday lives, noise we may sometimes create for our partner unless we are careful. In a sense, both individuals in a marriage are dependent on each other for the quietness required to explore that inner region. It was Rainer Maria Rilke who said it so thoughtfully: "A good marriage is that in which each appoints the other guardian of his solitude. Once the realization is accepted that even between the closest human beings infinite distances continue to exist, a wonderful living side-by-side can grow up, if they succeed in loving the distance between them that makes it possible for each to see the other whole against a wide sky."

• *Genuine love provides the freedom to share your real, authentic self with your partner.* Two people who enthusiastically share their individual discoveries about themselves can hardly keep from loving each other. For it is in the sharing of the deepest and most central parts of ourselves that we allow another person to really know us. The more we are known, the more we can be loved. If only superficial things are known about us, we will be loved only superficially.

• *Companionate love requires trust—and trust requires trustworthiness.* We do not form attachments to persons we cannot trust, any more than we would scale a mountain with a frayed rope. I am convinced that there are several aspects to being trustworthy. First, we need to trust our partner to be genuinely interested in us—in our safety and growth and success. Second, we need to trust that our partner will keep promises and avoid compromises that would damage the relationship. And third, becoming trustworthy requires unconditional love. It is this level of trust that makes for generous and genuine love that will withstand the test of time.

• *People who love each other well have shared dreams and plans for reaching them.* In other words, couples who dream great dreams together tend to love each other most. And when they strategize about how to reach their dreams, they are frequently the happiest. I often ask couples contemplating marriage, "Where do the two of you want to be in 10 or 20 years?" When they begin to speak, I can tell whether or not they have talked about the future. If they have both dreams *and* plans for realizing them, I have a strong inkling they're going to make it.

## How Can a Couple Develop Companionate Love?

Most couples know well the experience of passionate love. It comes naturally, instinctively. It requires no effort—it just happens. But most often, companionate love is not that way. It takes work. If a couple has experienced passionate love, how do they develop this deeper and richer kind of love?

There's a magic that some people seem to have when it comes to building love into their relationships. These purveyors of love seem capable of enriching not only romantic relationships but friendships and acquaintances as well.

I'll explain the characteristics of this deep love by describing a master of love. Marnie Fredericksen was my administrative assistant for several years while I was dean of a graduate school. She was so accomplished at loving people that when she retired, all of her co-workers recognized that a greatness had been present among us, the likes of which we might never see again. Let me tell you what I observed about her secrets of loving—both in relation to her husband, Vern, and virtually everyone else who came near her.

First, Marnie had the ability to make you feel that what counted most was *you*—not the scores of other people who clamored for her counsel, not the piles of paper she needed to process—only *you*. And it was genuine, not just a show. She focused her complete attention on the person she was with at the moment.

Marnie also listened so carefully that you sensed she knew exactly what you were feeling, thinking and trying to say. Sometimes I felt like she understood what I was trying to say better than I did, and that was a bit scary. When she heard me so well that my self-centeredness became obvious to her sensitive ears—and only later to my own—I wondered if her love for me would diminish. But that was never the case. When she decided to love someone, there were no conditions. That's another universal principle of companionate love—the ability to love unconditionally, accepting others as they are.

I also noticed that Marnie never failed to respond truthfully. If she thought you had made a mess of things, she let you know—but in a way that left your worth intact. Even when correcting or pointing out an error, Marnie gave you the feeling she loved *you*, even if she didn't approve of your performance. After a while, I realized she could tell the truth so pointedly, yet gently, because she loved the internal parts of people, not the external. She had the ability to look beyond outward flaws and focus on inward qualities.

One of the things Marnie did to love people—all kinds of people—was to "work" for them. If you had a need, she quietly tried to help meet it. She would figure out how to assist the people she loved. I saw her do it routinely for Vern and for her three daughters. She didn't have to say how much she loved these four people; she *showed* it by the way she served them. Amazingly, she loved and worked for all of our students and faculty in the same way. But when I received from her, I never got the feeling I left her depleted. She seemed to enjoy giving to others; she knew how to have a good time while taking care of the people she loved.

Finally, Marnie was an interpersonal genius. She could respond to the needs of people with uncanny efficiency. She had so mastered human nature that she usually knew how to diagnose and repair virtually any problem presented to her. She started with a deep respect for truth. She moved to the crux of the problem and confronted it squarely. "What's the real problem here?" was her approach. "And then," as Janie Elson, one of the persons who worked with Marnie, once said, "the magic would begin." Marnie would focus on *the* person in the midst of ringing telephones and every kind of interruption. Once focused, she listened intently to that person's story, wrapped her mind around the specific need, looked squarely at any issue that needed to be confronted, said just the right thing, threw in a little humor, developed a strategy to untangle the knots and gracefully exited with the problem solved.

Couples considering marriage should follow Marnie's example of love. Companionate love involves two people who know how to focus specifically on each other, listen long and carefully, and understand one another on a deep level. They discover each other's internal worlds, and they learn to love each other for qualities that are basically unchanging. They overlook defects and focus on attributes. Finally, they go to work in an effort to help each other solve problems and reach goals. That is what it means to be "in love." It is a quality of relating that is more important than any other because it is richer and more permanent. It is this kind of companionate love on which a successful marriage can be founded.

If you want to be involved in a love relationship that has substance, depth and real meaning, it is crucial that you recognize the skill involved. Marnie has incredible skills—*learned* skills. If you want to, you can transition from passionate love to a richer kind of love. But most of us are not natural lovers. We have to work at it. If it isn't automatic for you, consider yourself in good company. All kinds of people have turned ordinary relational skills into remarkable abilities. But it took work! And if you're willing to work, it can happen for you.

If this kind of love is not developed, relationships cannot survive for long. Most marriages fail due to an absence of companionate love. While I am optimistic about any couple being able to learn to love each other like this, the fact remains that an overwhelming percentage of all relationships never transition into this deeper kind of love.

In 1990, the Roper Institute surveyed 3,000 women and 1,000 men selected randomly from across America. These people were asked, "What makes a good marriage?" Out of all the answers given, one was most common for both sexes. "Being in love" was the answer given by 87 percent of the woman and 84 percent of the men.

It is clear that "being in love" involves significantly more than passion and romance. It is the deep, woven-together quality of two people who have developed a many-sided relationship. It is the knowledge these people have that they are cherished and honored and loved by their partner.

This kind of love can energize a marriage and fill it with vitality and health. It can create a relational fabric that will make life supremely worth living— even when problems arise. When this love develops for two people, they are ready to pledge themselves for a lifetime. But until it actually exists, wedding plans are premature. Marriage would be as risky as jumping from a skyscraper with 10 birthday balloons strapped to your back. "Passionate" love is exciting and wonderful, but "companionate" love is what makes a marriage successful.

# SEVEN
# Master the Art of Intimacy

Without question, the most important quality in a great marriage is intimacy. It is to romance what April showers and the sunshine of May are to a farmer's crops. When you are intimate with the person you love, you create unlimited possibilities for the growth of your relationship. Intimacy has the potential for lifting the two of you out of the lonely world of separateness and into the stratosphere of emotional oneness.

Conversely, the number one enemy of any marriage is a lack of intimacy. If two people do not know each other deeply, they can never become what the Bible calls "one flesh." They will never be "bonded," "fused," "merged" or "welded together." Without intimacy, they will be isolated and alone—even while living under the same roof.

When I speak to groups of singles and young couples, I frequently find they misunderstand what I mean by intimacy. Sometimes people assume I'm talking about sex. Others think I'm referring to "love talk," the warm expressions of affection and admiration. Certainly, a healthy sex life and good communication are parts of the intimacy equation—but only parts.

The kind of intimacy I talk about involves the sharing of that which is *innermost* for two people, their deepest thoughts, feelings, dreams, fears and joys. It is when this "core" information is revealed that partners become acquainted with each other's inner workings. In this process of discovery, they gain vital information about whether the two of them belong together permanently.

## Why Doesn't Intimacy Happen Very Often?

Many couples enter marriage without really knowing each other. Oh sure, they have discussed life histories, goals for the future, how many children they would like to have, and so on. As important as this information is, they may not be aware of the deep-down drives, motivations, fears and joys that comprise their partner's emotional foundation. If their relationship were an elevator, we might say they have stopped at the first floor, refusing to descend into the basement.

I am intrigued by the research of Dr. John Cuber, whose findings were published in the book *The Significant Americans*. Cuber studied scores of couples who remained married for one reason or another—some for the benefit of the children, others merely for physical companionship, and a few because they genuinely enjoyed each other. He found that only a small minority of couples experience real intimacy. Why is intimacy so hard to come by in a man-woman relationship?

First, it's not a skill that most families teach their children during the developmental years. Life is so fast paced that there isn't much opportunity to sit down for long periods and communicate. Most individuals don't have time to figure out what's really going on inside themselves—let alone take time to share it with others.

The escalating divorce rate also greatly impacts intimacy. The fact is that 70 percent of the children in our country will be involved with divorce at some time in their lives—either their parents' divorce or their own. When a family breaks apart, the lack of intimacy may well be a *cause*, and it almost always is a *consequence*.

Second, our society is relatively blind to the importance of intimacy, so there is little reward or reinforcement for those who master this art form. People are paid more in our society if they *produce* well, given prestige if they get *educated* and deemed valuable if they *look good*. But people who are able to communicate intimately with others are given little special recognition. Sometimes they are even ridiculed.

Third, intimacy requires a careful exploration of one's own inner world, and that's too frightening for some people. In our country there has been an epidemic of inattentiveness to the authentic, inner self, making intimacy virtually impossible. How can two people share their innermost emotions when they have fearfully refrained from looking deeply into themselves? They can't. Consequently, couples often settle for superficial relationships, leaving them essentially unmerged, setting themselves up to be blown apart when relatively mild storms come along.

# *Self-Discovery:*
# *The First Step Toward Intimacy*

I remember when Dennis and Jody came to me for counseling five years ago. Jody refused to marry Dennis, and he was angry about it. She had told Dennis that without some counseling, she didn't think they would ever build the kind of relationship she could commit to for a lifetime. Dennis came to me for one reason—to placate Jody so she would marry him.

During our first session, Jody outlined the problem: "Dennis and I never talk about anything important. He doesn't like to talk about what he calls 'the personal stuff.' Sometimes I'm so locked out of his life that I feel desperate. I start asking him all kinds of questions, and at first he gives me one-word answers. As my frustration grows, I talk louder and ask more questions. Finally, Dennis gets mad and tells me these things are personal and none of my business. Basically, he tells me to butt out. I just boil when he says that! I feel like a stranger with him. How can I marry someone I communicate with so little?"

I asked Dennis how he responded to all of that. "Well, it's true that we don't talk much about the things Jody wants to talk about," he replied. "But to tell you the truth, most of the time I don't know how to answer her questions. She asks me how I feel about this or that, and I don't *know* how I feel. She pushes me for my position on something, and I don't have the slightest idea what my position is. She wants to know where I'm headed in life, and I tell her I'll find out when I get there. Why worry about the future?"

Dennis was a veritable stranger to himself! How could he share his deepest thoughts, dreams and plans with Jody? He had no idea what they were himself!

You have to know yourself if you're going to be intimate with someone else. And the time to start being in touch with yourself is when you're born! That's only possible if someone older and wiser helps you. Your ability to be intimate with others depends largely on how your parents (or caregivers) raised you.

Here's what wise parents do to foster intimacy: They make it safe to get in touch with what you feel and think. They don't base your worth on whether or not they like what you're thinking or feeling. They may require certain *behaviors*, but they don't demand that you feel or think a certain way. In fact, by their interest and understanding, they help you identify what's going on inside of you. Healthy parents also encourage you to recognize your thoughts and emotions at any given moment. It's in your early years that you become knowledgeable about yourself, an expert on your insides. It is this kind of self-awareness that is such a critical part of intimacy.

Unfortunately, many children aren't lucky enough to have parents like that. What then? What if your parents failed to assist you in learning about the deepest parts of yourself? What happens to the person who reaches adolescence and has not developed this skill? This is where good friends come in. Many times, peers will make up for the absence of intimacy in the family.

Parents sometimes complain about their teenager's constant use of the phone. But these seemingly endless phone conversations may serve a useful purpose. If teenagers "process life" together, encouraging each other to discover their inner worlds, then the cost of all these calls will be infinitesimally small. Adolescents who talk on the phone or hang out at the park with friends may be acquiring skills that will be critical to their marriage later on. They are learning about who they are and how to share that knowledge with others.

Still, a lot of people go through childhood and adolescence without learning about themselves. Perhaps their families didn't emphasize self-discovery and they weren't blessed with friends who communicated at a deep level. Many of these young adults—and sometimes older adults—will try to develop intimacy skills in a dating relationship. Some people hope that with the help of their boyfriend or girlfriend they will be able to discover their deeper self.

However, I suspect this doesn't happen very often. There is simply too much at stake in a dating relationship. If a person is new to the process of intimacy, opening up for the first time with such an important person may create so much anxiety that the door to the inner world will remain locked.

I'm *not* saying that you can't learn to be intimate with the help of a trusted friend or sibling. These relationships sometimes provide enough safety and confidence to explore your inner self. But in a *romantic* relationship, there are usually so many emotions involved that it's difficult to test the waters of intimacy and vulnerability. Learning how to be intimate with someone is a major task. When there is so much at stake, the task may be ignored. It's simply too risky.

So it is that many—perhaps most—people reach adulthood never having learned how to be intimate. Some of these people have excelled in their careers, but their family lives are a mess. Some have amazing intellect but remain ignorant about the inner workings of their emotional life. Their lack of knowledge about who they are leaves them helpless to develop intimacy.

When people ask me how they can learn to be intimate, I make several suggestions. First, psychotherapy is all about intimacy—the discovery of oneself in the context of a meaningful relationship with a trusted guide. A skilled therapist or counselor can uncover roadblocks to intimacy and provide a safe environment for self-discovery.

Others may benefit from a therapy group. These groups allow their members to relive family situations and discuss their daily interactions. Fellow group members serve as a mirror, reflecting back what they see to help clarify thoughts and behaviors.

Sometimes I refer people to 12-step groups or church groups that emphasize growth and self-understanding. Most often, these are geared for "fellow strugglers," people with similar problems, and there is often strong accountability and encouragement.

Frequently, I simply give people exercises to complete. I strongly encourage them to keep a daily journal, write out their feelings and thoughts for a half hour each day, schedule times of reflection and prayer, and role-play various situations with others. This "mind and spirit homework" helps uncover memories, sort out thoughts and explore feelings.

# Intimacy Requires a Desire to Know Others

I recall a time early in our marriage when my wife, our firstborn child and I traveled by car across Wyoming. Marylyn and I had been married for three years, and we were still learning about each other. While our little girl slept in the back seat, Marylyn and I talked late into the night—partly to stay awake and partly to deepen our understanding of each other.

I will never forget my exhilaration in response to Marylyn's eager desire to know me better. "Just talk to me about you," she would say. No one had ever wanted to know me like that, and in the process of sharing myself with her, I came to understand myself much better.

For there to be real intimacy, two people must have a strong desire to know each other. But it's often how that desire is expressed that matters. I've found that four conditions usually must be met before others will share themselves at a deep level with you.

• *Interest.* People must be assured you really want to hear from them. If you don't, you won't need to say so. It will become evident very quickly. Your attention will wander, your eye contact will break, you may grow restless or your need for sleep may become apparent. Who wants to reveal vulnerable information about themselves when their listener isn't interested? Studies on intimate sharing indicate that "not really listening" is the most fundamental error people make. Perhaps this contributes to their tendency to interrupt, pick out small points to criticize and impatiently fail to wait for "the whole story."

• *Commitment.* The very deepest kind of sharing can take place only when there's no fear of rejection or abandonment. People need to know you are committed to the relationship before they'll open up. For honest interchanges to occur, there must be safety and security in the relationship. When true commitment exists, both persons feel free to dialogue about anything and everything.

• *Camaraderie.* People who reveal their emotions need to know you genuinely like them. The other day, a client suddenly stopped in the middle of our first session together and said: "I need to know if you like me. Do you?" It was the exact question she needed to ask, because if I didn't like her, it would be risky for her to share deeply with me.

• *Participation.* Persons who genuinely love each other and seek a deep relationship actively participate in the intimacy process. They sit forward, maintain eye contact, ask probing questions and guide the discussion with comments. Intimacy happens best when two people listen carefully to each other, convey their support to one another, and totally refrain from judging and blaming.

# *Intimacy Involves*
# *Shared Emotions and Experiences*

It's wonderful to share something extremely personal and have someone say, "I know exactly what you mean" or "That's happened to me, too" or "That's how I've always felt." This is an experience of infinite delight that cements two people together. In such moments, kindred spirits are discovered.

Intimacy is impossible without at least a thread of shared emotions, experiences or beliefs. The more commonalities there are, the deeper intimacy can go.

It is one thing to find that you and your lover share some superficial interests in common, like homing pigeons or stamp collecting. But it is quite another thing to find that something you thought was totally unique to you is shared by your partner. It's a powerful experience to communicate intensely with someone who knows precisely how you think and feel.

I recently went to lunch with Dr. Jokichi Takamine, a past president of the Los Angeles County Medical Association. We got to talking about intimacy and self-disclosure, and we zeroed in on the commonalities and shared beliefs that make a marriage great.

We found ourselves constantly returning to the importance of *spirituality*. When two people discover that they have a spiritual hunger or spiritual awareness in common, they are strongly drawn to one another. In fact, I have found that a lack of mutually held spiritual beliefs often signals an intimacy deficit that leaves couples dangerously unconnected. In fact, one research study showed that spirituality ranked among the six most common characteristics of strong families. The strongest families in this study reported experiencing "a sense of power and a purpose" greater than themselves—*a spiritual orientation.*[1]

A woman came to me recently from across the country. She had been married for seven years when her husband left her, and she spent the next two years trying to get him back. Even though he didn't ask for a divorce, he consistently refused to come home. Recently, he called her out of the blue, wanting to come home immediately. He said he had finally realized how much he needs her and wants her. He would move back tomorrow!

Although this woman didn't want to turn her husband away, especially after all she did to get him back, she now doubts that their marriage can work. I explored this conclusion with her extensively. Here is what she told me: "When I'm with him, we simply don't have much intimacy. He makes all kinds of money, but we can't talk about the things that matter most to me. He has absolutely no interest in my deepest thoughts and feelings—the spiritual part of me. I can't be married to a person who is a stranger to the most essential part of who I am—however good looking or rich he is."

When two people have this spiritual dimension in common, it makes up for other areas of separateness. Sometimes people get married after having negative "religious" experiences as kids. They want to throw religion over and pretend it doesn't exist. But in the process, they repress and deny everything in them that is at all "spiritual" and thereby close themselves off to some of the most profound parts of the human experience. The consequence of this strategy is a sense of emptiness and superficiality—both individually and maritally. I am convinced that countless marriages fail because of a lack of spiritual rootedness.

## When Is Intimacy Most Likely to Happen?

As I suggested earlier, intimacy requires three fundamental qualities— knowledge of one's own inner life, a strong desire to know the other person and the existence of shared emotions and experiences. Assuming that a man and woman have these qualities, there is one important factor still to be considered. It has to do with *setting*.

In what physical and emotional contexts is intimacy most likely to happen? If you know the answer to this question, you can increase the opportunities to cultivate heartfelt communication. I believe that intimacy is most likely to occur under the following conditions:

1. *When plenty of time is available.* Research studies indicate that marital happiness is highly correlated with the amount of time spent together. Under ordinary circumstances, intimacy does not often occur when two people are hurried. That is why the pace of life in our society makes intimacy so difficult to achieve. But when a couple is together on a Friday afternoon, with no plans or time constraints, intimacy becomes much more likely. When a relaxing holiday or a week of vacation comes along, the stage is set for heart-to-heart talks.

I wouldn't want you to infer that intimacy is possible *only* when there is a lot of time, but it's much more likely to occur when there's no fear of needing to cut a conversation short.

2. *When you're away from the routine.* Intimacy seems to get crowded out by day-to-day duties and distractions. There is something about the home and office grind that switches our brains to an action mode, often thwarting introspection.

You don't have to get very far away from that routine before you begin to relax and open your mind. It may be just a dinner across town or a drive to the country or an hour in the park. If you succeed in removing yourself from the usual routine, you will make intimacy far more likely.

3. *In times of crisis or pain.* I have often said that pain is a trustworthy teacher, but pleasure can easily lead us astray. This is certainly true in relation to intimacy. When we are in emotional or physical pain, we turn inward and examine what we feel and think. When we discover what's going on inside of us, we want to tell the people we love most. Even those who have little awareness of their internal processes are often willing to share their thoughts and feelings when faced with a crisis or tragedy.

That's one of the reasons lovers seem to grow closer when they go through painful experiences together. They encounter the deep parts of each other that are seldom apparent when life is untroubled and carefree.

4. *When couples are regularly involved in reflection and introspection.* Time alone to read and think, to ponder and pray, nearly always leads to deeper awareness. Couples who have a regular time of reflection excel at intimacy. If you get more deeply in touch with yourself, you always have more to give to the intimacy process. Spend consistent time plumbing the depths of your own internal world, and you may discover that your relationship with your partner will deepen.

# Intimacy Helps You Assess Your Relationship

Let me make something clear that has been implicit throughout this chapter. Intimacy does not *automatically* contribute to bonding and connectedness. When you are intimate with another person, you are sharing your innermost worlds, and in this process you become deeply known to each other. This awareness will either confirm a sense of oneness or highlight differences and separateness.

As a matter of fact, this is what makes intimacy so incredibly important— and so dangerous. When you discover shared emotions and viewpoints, a binding together occurs that makes you feel you were meant for each other. You experience a joining that has an eternal quality to it—like it has always been so and always will be.

However, deep sharing may lead you to realize you *don't* feel or think alike. If these differences are significant enough, they may cast a shadow of doubt over your relationship. If this occurs, you should carefully consider your future together. Trying to force two lives together—lives that are fundamentally quite different—is the very thing that leads to unhappy and unsuccessful marriages.

When two people share deeply about themselves, they can begin to evaluate seriously whether their relationship can last a lifetime. This is why intimacy is so important for any couple considering a permanent relationship. They have an opportunity to see each other at the deepest levels and assess the degree to which they are alike. They can evaluate whether or not they will be able to live their lives in harmony and peace.

# EIGHT
# Learn How to Clear Conflict From the Road of Love

Paul and Betty told me that they have never had a single fight—not even a tiny argument. They claimed to get along perfectly, and they expected their flawless track record to continue once they got married.

As I sat listening to them, I thought, *What's wrong with these two? Why are they trying so hard to avoid conflict?* It made me nervous that they were getting married without knowing much about a critical aspect of their relationship. They didn't have the slightest idea about their combined ability to manage conflict.

Disagreements and quarrels in a relationship are inevitable, and they can be beneficial or deadly. If two people know how to resolve conflicts so that their relationship deepens and matures, they possess a magnificent skill. But if they don't know how to deal effectively with their disagreements, their marriage may be systematically destroyed. In my opinion, more marriages fail because two people don't know how to handle their differences than any other reason. That's why it's so vital to know ahead of time that you and your spouse-to-be are skillful at managing problems. If you don't know that, you're taking an awful risk in getting married.

# Can Conflict Actually Contribute to a Marriage?

Most people assume that *no* conflict means their relationship is better than if they have *some* conflict. But I don't think so. Of course, when there are *a lot* of disagreements between two people, they may be too different, and perhaps they should consider not forming a marriage.

But the best relationships I know are ones in which both people are fully open and authentic, and they cannot be that way without discovering their differences. These dissimilarities represent the unique perspectives that they each bring to the relationship. And even though these differences may need to be resolved, it is in the act of resolution that a couple can come to know and respect each other more deeply.

The degree to which any couple can allow for openness and authenticity is the degree to which their relationship will be complete and satisfying. If they hide their thoughts and feelings out of fear that conflict may result, it won't be long until they feel a sense of inner lostness and resentment toward each other.

Good relationships allow for a considerable amount of individual freedom for one of two reasons. The partners may discover in their openness that they are very much alike, perhaps because of cultural and genetic similarities. Or they may discover that the two of them, even though they have differences, *have learned to manage these differences to the ultimate advantage of their relationship*. It is this skill that every couple needs to develop before they marry. Otherwise, they cannot be confident about the durability of their partnership.

# The Foundational Secret of Successful Conflict Resolution

When I first met Russ and Jamie, I was impressed with the way they related to each other. We weren't a half hour into their first premarital counseling session when I came to believe they could resolve most any difference.

I talk to myself at times like this: *What am I picking up that makes me so sure this couple can handle the problems they are bound to encounter?* Sometimes I'm startled at the simplicity of my internal response: *They respect themselves, and they respect each other.* I know that constructive conflict revolves around mutual respect, and harmful conflict almost always involves at least one person's insecure preoccupation with individual needs.

But how do I know, after just a short time, how much respect persons have for themselves and each other? Partly because I've learned what to look for. Here is how I determine whether they respect themselves: I listen carefully when I ask them questions. Do they check inside themselves for the answers and take time to formulate these answers? Do they seem satisfied with their formulations when they finish? Do they state their opinions with assurance? If they do, they likely trust and respect themselves.

I also watch the person who is *not talking* to see how much attention that person pays to his or her partner. I observe the facial expressions and the amount of eye contact that is maintained. This tells me how much partners respect each other.

People respect each other by the way they speak and listen to one another, the way they touch, and the way they bring each other into the conversation. How two people treat each other when there is no conflict is the best predictor of how they will respond when conflict occurs. And if I come to believe they respect themselves *and* each other, I become confident they can resolve virtually *any* conflict they encounter. It's that simple!

You may wonder if I have oversimplified the foundation for conflict resolution. Let me tell you more about Russ and Jamie. I asked them how happy their childhoods were. They spoke honestly about the mostly positive experiences they had as children, but they also told of some negative times. Through all of this, they listened to each other like they had never heard the other person tell the story before.

Then I asked about their relationships with their parents. Clinical experience suggests that a person's parental relationships—especially with the mother—are crucial for predicting how effectively he or she will succeed in marriage.

"She was such a simple, caring person," Russ said about his mother. "She was one of nine children, and her family lived on a farm. She only went through the eighth grade, but she had good basic skills in reading and writing. She never had much self-esteem and never helped me with my school work, but she always pulled for me and cheered my accomplishments."

Russ paused for nearly a minute, obviously reflecting on his experiences with his mother. "I suppose the thing I remember most about her," he continued, "were the times she used to get up with me in the middle of the night when I had earaches. I was in the fifth or sixth grade at the time. She would hold my head on her lap and do everything she could to comfort me." Tears filled his eyes, and he was too choked up to talk anymore.

Jamie didn't say a word. She just reached over and took hold of his hand. All through his story, Jamie's eyes were focused on his. She listened with the kind of respect I know to be foundational for conflict resolution.

Conflict is a thousand times easier to manage if two people deeply respect themselves and each other. If that foundation is present, the techniques of conflict resolution can be learned easily. But if respect is not present, all the techniques in the world will not be enough.

# *Five Simple Techniques*
# *for the Mastery of Conflict*

Once we have established that a couple has the kind of respect I've just described, we can talk about some techniques for managing differences. There are five proven ways to resolve conflict. If a couple like Russ and Jamie will practice these, eventually making them automatic, no conflict will be able to defeat them.

**1.** *There must be a basic agreement that both people have a legitimate right to feel and think the way they do.* No one is wrong simply because he or she disagrees with the other person or does things differently.

I find it crucial in the early phases of a relationship to acknowledge this point over and over. There is something wonderful about being told by your partner, "I disagree with you, but you have a legitimate right to think and feel the way you do." This substantially reduces the threat of feeling *wrong* just because you're *different.* That's a troubling feeling that can result in defensiveness and combativeness.

**2.** *Both persons need to be fully heard by their partner, and they need to know they have been accurately understood.* It's more important for me to be heard and understood than to win a point. If I *know* that the other person understands my thoughts and feelings, I almost automatically feel relieved even if our differences continue.

The technique I have found to be most helpful in this regard was originally proposed by Dr. Carl Rogers, a famous American psychologist. It goes like this: Each partner is required to put into his or her own words what the other person has said before making the next comment. Reflecting your partner's feelings and thoughts like this contributes surprisingly to the resolution process.

I never cease to be impressed with what happens when my wife, Marylyn, and I run into conflict. We have a tendency to repeat our points over and over, hoping that the obvious superiority of our position will finally become persuasive. Sometimes it occurs to one of us (along about midnight) that it might be helpful to understand out loud exactly what the other person is saying. "Okay now, Marylyn," I might say, "let me see if I understand what you are saying. You believe that . . ." And then I explicate her position as accurately as I can. All of a sudden, there is a totally different feel about our conflict. And almost before we know it, we are moving toward resolution.

**3.** *Your points of disagreement need to be specified carefully, and then agreed upon.* It can be hard to define the problems, so sometimes it is best to do this in writing.

Most conflict occurs over *minor* disagreements. Imagine for a moment that you and your potential partner are arguing about what you are going to do tonight. He wants to go to a professional basketball game, but you want to rent a movie.

"I want to go to the game," he says, "because it will determine whether the Knicks make the playoffs. You know I'm a big fan, and this is a crucial game. I want to be with you, and I want to see that game."

"But wait," you say, "I'm beat. This has been an exhausting week, and I just need to stay home. I want to rent a movie, fix a simple dinner at my place, and watch the movie with you in front of a fire."

As the argument builds, new dimensions keep emerging. You say tickets for the game will be too expensive, and there might not be any tickets available by the time you get there. He says that you never want to go anywhere lately, that you are tired a lot, that you and he can watch the movie anytime.

Here's where conflict-resolution skill number three comes in. Together, specify your differences: (1) Basketball game versus movie; (2) Staying home versus going out; (3) Spending a lot of money versus being thrifty. You've cleared away the other points that confuse things and identified the root issues. Then you're ready for the next skill.

**4.** *An attitude of "give and take" greatly facilitates resolution.* You need to say something like this to each other: "Let's see, where can I give and where can you give so we can move toward one another?" When a couple says this, they are on the threshold of actually *benefiting* from their conflict. This statement conveys an attitude of compromise, an obvious desire for both persons to be winners. There is a willingness to change in order to obtain a mutually satisfying final result. It's wonderful to be "partnered" with somebody who wants you to be a winner without being a loser himself.

Here's the kind of thing you might say about the movie-basketball game impasse: "I know how much you want to see the game, and you're right, we can watch this movie anytime. Would you feel okay about coming over to my place tonight and watching the game on TV with me?" And I can imagine him saying: "Yeah, I guess that would be okay. I'd love to go to the game, but I know you're tired. Let me stop and get some pizza on the way over so you don't have to cook."

About now you may be saying: "C'mon, Neil, this is too easy! It just doesn't happen that neatly. Your compromises are too 'perfect' to fit a real argument."

Let me share one response before I propose the final conflict-resolution skill. Conflicts are often *easily* resolved *if* the partners' basic attitudes toward each other are healthy, positive and loving. Conflict becomes dangerous and difficult when one or both persons feel uncared for, misunderstood and minimized. When you sense that the person you love is eager to resolve a difference in a way that will leave you both feeling good, you become cooperative. But you'll probably become combative if you feel he or she wants to win and hardly cares about what you want.

**5.** *When you resolve a conflict with your partner, congratulate each other.* Praise the person you love for the qualities that allowed both of you to get your needs met and feel important in the process.

My wife and I have an ongoing conflict that revolves around the temperature in our home. I guess my internal thermometer is more extreme than hers. I like it warmer in the winter and cooler in the summer than she does. This frustrates her, because it means our gas bill goes up in the winter more than she thinks is necessary, and then our electric bill does the same in the summer. We try to compromise to maintain the peace between us and keep us comfortable.

But one night, while Marylyn went to bed early, I stayed up late to watch a delayed telecast of the UCLA-Oregon basketball game. Around midnight, I realized that the room was very warm—even warmer than I like it. But I didn't do anything about it because I was so engrossed in the game. Eventually, I went on to bed without checking the thermostat.

The next morning, she said, "Part of the reason we didn't sleep very well last night is because the heat was left on so high. I had turned it way up so it would be nice and warm when you came home from work."

I was deeply touched by that, and I said: "I'm really sorry that I left it on so high. I was excited about the game, and I just went right by the thermostat without even checking it." Then I said what had touched me: "That was so loving of you to have turned the heat up so I would feel warm at dinner."

I tell this whole story to get to her response, which is a good example of conflict-resolution skill number five. It didn't come until that evening. She said in a casual moment: "That was wonderful the way you handled the matter about the heat. I thought about it several times today at work." That's all she said, and it made me want to create some more conflict right then so I could handle it "wonderfully" again. It made me feel a whole new burst of love for her. Imagine! I felt all that simply because she reinforced me for the way I had reinforced her. We had managed conflict in a way that left both of us feeling more loved *by* and more loving *toward* the other person.

As simple as these five conflict-resolution skills are, there are countless couples who continue to ignore them—and suffer severe relational consequences. If you're in a relationship in which you and your potential spouse regularly disagree, and you both seem unable to implement these five constructive processes, I strongly suggest that you delay getting married. First, prove to each other that as a couple you are capable of automatically practicing these ways of managing conflict.

# The Most Common Ways to Mismanage Conflict

I have concluded that most of the couples I see for premarital counseling have no idea how to manage conflict. When you combine this conclusion with my earlier statement that an inability to resolve conflict can devastate a relationship, it is easy to understand why so many marriages are failing today.

There are four principal ways in which people mismanage marital conflict:

• *Denial.* Some people are so convinced that conflict is necessarily destructive that they refuse to even acknowledge it in themselves. Like the couple I mentioned at the beginning of this chapter, they simply *never* fight, argue or even disagree.

But one thing is certain: It is impossible to erase resentment—even if you fail to recognize conflict. And when you deny the conflict and try to remove it from your awareness, the effects are sometimes much more devastating than when the experience is completely conscious. I can't begin to tell you the number of married couples I have counseled through the years who were ready to call it quits because their marriages had become frozen, even though they had seldom had any conscious disagreements.

A man from Arkansas called me the other day to say his marriage of 28 years had ended in divorce recently. "People were stunned when they found out," he told me, "because my wife and I never argued or fought with each other." I wasn't too surprised; I've seen too many marriages like his that just "cracked apart" from within. I asked this man how he explained why this had happened.

"My folks fought violently with each other all through my childhood," he said, "and when I was 14, I promised myself I would never fight with my wife."

"But wasn't that frustrating for your wife?" I asked him. "No," he said, "her folks never fought, and her mother died when she was 15 years old. She was totally unfamiliar with conflict and how to resolve it."

Hear my warning: Be wary of marrying anyone whose parents never had *any* disagreements—*or* whose parents fought violently. Your potential partner may have learned conflict-resolution styles exactly like his or her parents—or exactly the opposite. In either case, he or she learned all the wrong ways to handle the difficult parts of a relationship.

Likewise, be *very* wary of marrying someone who seems determined never to recognize differences between you. This is *denial,* and it will render you unable to remove from the road to love the debris that unresolved conflict always leaves behind.

• *Nonengagement.* A person who recognizes conflict in the relationship but refuses to discuss it has adopted a very destructive style called *nonengagement.* The difference between nonengagement and denial is awareness.

These people simply will not engage in conflict, but they will let their displeasure be known in other ways. They may pout, give you the silent treatment, carefully avoid conflictual topics or punish you by maintaining emotional distance. These approaches are terribly destructive. If you try to break through them, there is usually a second level of defense—and maybe even a third. Let me give you an example.

I know a woman who has never argued with her husband. She simply won't engage. It's obvious when she's upset; she goes completely silent and totally shuts her husband out. Her silence is deafening! If he tries to ask her about it, she simply stays quiet. It's a punishment he has grown to detest, and it has nearly destroyed their marriage.

Why does she do it? I asked her that, and she even gave me permission to print her response:

> My husband and I have never been able to settle any differences
> we have. If I tell him I am upset about something, he yells at me. I
> am devastated by his yelling, and I have decided never to trigger it
> again. It works far better for me just to be quiet.

This woman has adopted a style of nonengagement in an effort to manage her husband's anger. She has given up finding a way to work through conflict with him. Their marriage has to weave its way through the rubble of dozens of disagreements that have never been resolved.

• *Anger explosion.* I have dealt with more than 400 "anger mismanagers" over the years, and I know these people well. Persons who regularly explode are a breed to themselves. Psychologists used to think they were nearly all men, but that's not completely true. Now we know that men usually explode at their wives, and women explode at their children.

These people are frightening! I have watched some of them actually hit their spouse or children in my office. *Time* magazine says that four to six million spouses and millions of children are beaten up in the United States every year by the people who profess to love them the most.

Why do they do this? Obviously, it *never* gets them what they really want. They want to be listened to and respected. They want to have their opinions and feelings count. Their angry outbursts almost never have this consequence, but they seem to get what they want for a little while. They explode over and over again because of the reinforcement they experience during the time they are doing it—and for a few minutes afterward.

What is this reinforcement? They feel such a sense of power and validation when all that adrenaline is pumping through their systems. When they are shouting and pounding and spitting their words out, they actually think they are getting some respect, that they are in charge and doing something that will benefit them. But quite the opposite is true!

Unfortunately, a lot of people are addicted to this style of handling conflict, and if they fail to obtain professional help, they will likely continue this way forever.

• *Manipulation*. This can take many different forms. Let me name a few:

**1**. Guilt: "Now, honey, Grandma is getting very old, and you should just do as she says. She may not live much longer."

**2**. Flattery: "It would be *such* an honor for me if someone of your significance were to do that for me."

**3**. Threats: "If you don't want to accompany me to the party, I'm sure there are a lot of other women who would love to go with me."

**4**. Blackmail: "If you'll do this, I won't tell Dad what you did with the gift he gave you."

**5**. Subtle deal-making: "I know what I'm asking turns you off, but if you'll go ahead and do it, I think you'll be glad you did."

**6.** Blatant pay-off: "If you'll go along with me on this one, I'll do what you want on that other one."

When you encounter a prospective partner who uses devious manipulations to get his or her way, be very careful. Manipulation in any form robs you of your dignity and creates within you a sense of being coerced and managed. These people simply want *their* way; they want you to give in, and they will try almost anything to reach their goal. And if one manipulation doesn't work, they will try another one.

# Why Do Some Couples Benefit From Conflict, While Others Are Destroyed By It?

By now you know I believe that conflict is inevitable for any two people committed to being free and authentic in their relationship. And I further believe that conflict can be either destructive or helpful. It all depends on how it is handled. If it is not handled at all, or not handled well, it can destroy a relation-ship. But if it is managed carefully and thoughtfully, it can help build a deeper and more satisfying partnership.

So what is it about a couple that determines which route they will take? In my experience with couples dealing with conflict resolution, I have identified certain factors that place a couple in one of two groups.

Couples who handle conflict destructively usually exhibit the following pattern:

**1.** One or both persons grew up in a home in which conflict was handled poorly or never handled at all.

**2.** They now believe that conflict is dangerous, that it is better left un-acknowledged. Or when they try to deal with it, they are awkward or harsh, and always ineffective.

**3.** Then there develops a commitment to keeping the peace by denying individual differences.

**4**. There is a sense on both their parts that the relationship should be kept superficial. There is a fear that they should not "venture into the deep."

**5**. When these people do have to confront conflict, they both feel ill at ease. They simply do not feel safe in the relationship when they are different from each other.

**6**. Because they each feel insecure, they tend to talk far too much and listen far too little.

**7**. Without even knowing it, they become committed to "winning" rather than "resolving" a conflict.

**8**. They each regularly feel misunderstood, stifled and disrespected. This reinforces the belief that conflict is bad for their relationship.

**9**. They tend to keep more things inside, to hide themselves from their partner.

**10**. As differences build between them, their first response is denial. If that succeeds, their relationship becomes more superficial. But if that fails, they become engaged in a manipulation battle with one another. When that fails, they either get outside help or their marriage flounders—or ends.

I recognize that this is a pessimistic analysis. But unfortunately, I've witnessed this pattern many times. That's why I believe so strongly that every couple considering marriage needs to assess carefully their combined abilities to handle differences. If an individual or a couple believes conflict can be ignored, disaster is almost certain.

Now for the good news. Some couples do handle conflict well. Here's how they typically go about it:

**1**. There is a strong commitment to harmony, but only if it involves openness and authenticity on the part of both individuals.

**2**. Both persons have a deep respect for themselves and for their partner.

**3**. Both persons expect there to be differences between them, and they welcome them.

**4**. There is a high appreciation for the uniqueness of the other person and an understanding of the importance of listening and hearing accurately.

**5.** Each person has a strong sense of comfort in the relationship.

**6.** There is a determination to *deal* with conflict, not ignore it.

**7.** Both people are able to admit when they are wrong.

**8.** There is a lack of defensiveness—an absence of competition and the desire to win.

**9.** There is an eagerness on both their parts to congratulate each other when differences are resolved happily.

**10.** There is a recognition that the road to love needs to be kept clear of conflict and resentment, and there is a willingness to spend the time required to get this done.

Any couple who can deal positively with conflict has a skill of tremendous value. I think Daniel Goleman of the *New York Times* was on the mark when he said: "The ability to talk over problems is more important than how much a couple is in love or how happy they were before the marriage."

When couples are unable to deal effectively with their differences, marriage is simply too risky for them. They need to wait until they have remedied their insufficiency. I remember counseling a premarital couple who was having a terrible time with conflict resolution. They argued about all kinds of things, and they even disagreed about how to approach their disagreements. The woman told me that he always had to win every argument, and the man told me that he usually ended up feeling responsible for every problem they had. I knew they were in deep trouble, and I recommended that they delay their marriage until they developed the skill to solve their problems in a way that left them both feeling good.

I strongly believe that any couple who wants a lasting marriage will have to learn how to manage conflict constructively. If they don't, the time will come when the road to love will be so littered with the garbage of unresolved disagreements that they will simply not be able to move ahead. Obviously, the best time to determine whether they have what it takes to keep that road open is well before settling on a wedding date.

# NINE
# Refuse to Proceed Until You Can Genuinely Pledge Your Lifelong Commitment

When I was a young parent of three little girls, I sometimes wondered whether I would ever be able to walk them down the wedding aisle without falling apart. I couldn't imagine putting one of their little hands into the hand of "another man" and watch her lock arms with a "stranger." Then I was supposed to stand there and say "her mother and I do" at just the right time. I knew my heart would break.

Years later, as Lorrie's wedding approached, the pressure grew. I worked through all the psychological principles I knew for the careful management of strong emotion in a public place. Then when I thought I could depend on myself not to make a scene, Lorrie and Greg asked me if I would "deliver the charge" to the two of them during the ceremony. I was going to have to stand in front of all those people, control all that emotion, and say a whole lot more than "her mother and I do."

I thought for days about what that "charge" should be. I wondered if I would ever get clear about what to say to my "little girl" and this "other man."

Then one afternoon when I was in my office between appointments, I laid my head back for a minute and closed my eyes. In my nervousness, I visualized standing in front of that big wedding party and all those other people. In my mind's eye I saw Greg's parents, Joe and Gerri Forgatch, right there on the front row. And I saw my wife across the aisle. Most everyone else was a blur, but then I saw my father and mother just behind my wife. I suddenly began to get a sense of what I should say to the bride and groom.

I began my charge like this: "Lorrie and Greg, a successful marriage and a healthy family require an old-fashioned, deep-down, lifelong commitment. It is my own mother and father who have taught me this principle most effectively. In two months, they will have been married for 70 years."

As I stood there that night with a bright, energetic young couple facing me and a wise 90-year-old twosome just to my right, I couldn't help but hope that the principles that had so successfully guided the veterans would become just as important to the rookies.

## *What Does Commitment Really Mean?*

It was on August 21st in the "summer of their youth" that my mom and dad *committed* themselves to each other. I know that date nearly as well as I know my own birthday, because in our family we celebrated it annually with great fanfare. Their lifetime pledge was monumental for us. It had not only led to their eating all those breakfasts together and having an infinite number of experiences in common, but it also made possible my two sisters and me, 12 grandchildren, 12 great-grandchildren and two great-great-grandchildren. They *pledged themselves* to each other "for as long as we both shall live," and their commitment of undying affection for each other gave birth to a physical and emotional security that radically influenced *everything* about their lives—and ours—*forever*.

Let's get right to the heart of the matter: What was the nature of their commitment? What does it mean to *commit* yourself to someone?

We can look at the traditional wedding vows for a clear understanding of what it is you are committing to. Usually, there is a single question to which you answer "I do," and then a specific vow that you say to your mate. The question is simply this:

James, do you take Susan to be your wife, and do you solemnly promise to love, honor and cherish her, and that forsaking all others for her alone, you will perform unto her all the duties that a husband owes to his wife until God by death shall separate you?

And the traditional wedding vow goes like this:

I, Susan, take you, James, to be my husband. And I promise and covenant before God and these witnesses to be your loving and faithful wife—in plenty and in want, in joy and in sorrow, in sickness and in health—as long as we both shall live.

So you commit yourself to:

1. Love your mate until one of you dies.

2. Honor your mate until one of you dies.

3. Cherish your mate until one of you dies.

4. Not be involved with *any* other "substitute mate."

5. Perform all the duties as a spouse until one of you dies.

6. Be *loving* and *faithful* through *every* kind of circumstance for as long as the two of you live.

*Is this a radical promise or not?*

I am asserting in this chapter that you *not* get married—that you absolutely *refuse* to even consider it—until you can genuinely make this kind of lifelong pledge to your mate. If you are not prepared to do so, then you are not ready to be married. Marriage is far too demanding, far too complex, to be taken on by anyone who is unsure of his or her determination to do *all* six of these things *forever*.

# Has Marriage Commitment Been Taken Seriously in Our Culture?

*No!* Obviously, we have trivialized marriage commitment! We have been so concerned about not limiting individual freedom that we have literally watched completely unprepared people walk into and out of marriages with hardly a frown on our faces. We have been so concerned about not trapping someone in a destructive relationship that we have opened wide the door to divorce and taught people that commitment for a lifetime is out-dated and irrelevant. As a society, we have taken the position that "commitment" is a cute, but insignificant, part of an overly idealistic view of marriage. We hold to it when it's convenient, and we ignore it when it's not.

I am convinced that our society's fundamental problem is the breakdown of the traditional family. And I'm further convinced that the family will never become structurally sound again until we begin to take seriously all that is involved in commitment.

It's commitment that makes trust possible. How can you trust someone if you know he or she is not determined to make your relationship work for a lifetime? And without deep trust, how can you share your innermost thoughts and feelings? How can you express everything from the deepest parts of you? If you can't do that, how strong can your marriage become? And without any lasting intimacy, can a couple provide the kind of emotional environment in which children can grow to be strong and healthy? I think you can see how easily a marriage lacking genuine commitment can fall apart like a house of cards.

# Has the Meaning of Commitment Been Misunderstood?

Yes! A lot of people think of commitment as "physical presence." That is, not leaving your spouse. But that is just a *minor* part of marriage commitment. I know two people who have stayed in their sick marriage for more than 20 years because, as they said, "that's what commitment is all about."

However, commitment asks a thousand times more of you than just to stay in the marriage! It asks that you *love, honor* and *cherish* the other person. It means avoiding a substitute spouse of any kind. It requires that you do everything in *your* power to be all that your role requires of you. And it asks that you do all of this through *every* kind of circumstance for as long as you live. This kind of commitment has simply *not* been understood in our society.

You will note that true commitment has not a whiff of conditionality about it, not a thread of mutuality and reciprocity in it. It does not depend on the degree to which your mate does it. You are committed to love and loyalty for a lifetime—no matter what!

I'm convinced that until we get this understanding of commitment back into focus, many marriages are going to be flimsy and unequal to the demands of living in these days.

## *The Role of Willpower*

When I talk to people considering marriage, I zero in on the crucial nature of *willpower*. In the final analysis, and not without a major struggle within me, I believe that love is a decision. I admit that it is tough to have to exert willpower and determination to love someone. It is so much easier when love flows naturally.

However, I learned a long time ago that most people, including me, go through times when we are not very lovable. We get beaten up by stress, discouraged by our lack of success, overburdened by work, underpaid, sick or whatever. For short or long periods of time, we need to be loved even though we don't merit it.

And I have watched people who are able to love the unlovable. Sometimes it's a spouse or a child or a close friend. These lovers just hang in there through all kinds of storms and problems in the life of the one they love.

I've often asked them how they do it, how they manage to stay so caring and loyal. The answers are usually similar: "I decided a long time ago that I love him, and once I decided that, nothing could change it." How can that be? How can they love through thick and thin, through bad times and good, and when the other person is negative and irritable and a mess?

It's a matter of the will! They decide to do it!

That's exactly what is required when it comes to marriage. You keep loving and cherishing and honoring and being true because you decide to, because you *will* it to be.

# Is It Often Hard to Keep Your Commitment?

*Hard?* Sometimes it seems impossible! Many people ask themselves: How can I keep loving and honoring and cherishing this person who is doing me wrong, being so irritable, offering so little, so frequently failing to keep his side of the bargain? How can I love her when she drinks so much? How can I love him when he comes home so late? How can I love her when she tells her parents all kinds of things about me? How can I love him when he gambles our food money away, when he won't look for a job, when he's on drugs, when he and his friends treat me so poorly? How can I love her when she yells at the kids? How can I love him when he is so stingy with me?

*Sometimes marriage is so difficult that commitment seems impossible!*

But, if it weren't hard, impossibly hard, why would there be any need for powerful and demanding marriage vows? We could just ask people to repeat something like this:

I, James, take you, Susan, to be my wife. I promise to love you whenever possible. When you are worthy of it, I will honor you.

134

When I want something from you and you give it to me, I will cherish you. If everything goes well between us, our relationship will continue. From my point of view it will mostly depend upon you, and I wish you nothing but the best.

# The Time to Think About Commitment

There is only *one* time to think about commitment—*before you make it!* That's what makes this mate-selection task so incredibly important. It is *before* you are married that this overwhelming commitment must be considered. After you have pledged yourself for a lifetime, your whole focus changes to how you can most effectively keep your commitment—how you can deeply love, honor and cherish your mate.

Please do not misunderstand how incredibly difficult I consider it to be to keep your commitment after you are married. I have listened to hundreds of couples who were struggling with this issue, and I have tried my hardest to help them keep on loving and cherishing and honoring when it was no longer natural. Sometimes it was simply not possible for them to do it without some kind of miracle. But I believe so strongly in the importance of keeping your commitment that it is well worth all the effort.

Many couples have told me it was impossible for them to keep their commitment because "this marriage was just not right from the very beginning." Hundreds of persons knew "right after their wedding" or "in the first month of their marriage" that their relationship was horribly wrong. And now they want out. They want to forget they ever said their vows.

Why is it that most of these people have children? This makes their decision to split up so much more destructive! No child survives the breakup of their parents' marriage without enormous hurt, which often never heals. Parents should not be able to have children unless they can prove to a jury of their peers that their marriage is incredibly healthy—and unless they will sign in blood a promise *never* to break their commitment.

All of this is to say that the time to consider commitment is before marriage. I tell the people who come to me, "Don't be afraid to walk away from the relationship at *any* time *before* you say your vows—even if it is while you are standing before a minister, priest or rabbi! But once you have made your commitment, make it work. Be a person of your word."

# Can You Ever Know Enough to Commit Yourself for a Lifetime?

This is a question that plagues me! Is it possible to know if a particular person is the right person for you—for the rest of your life? Can you ever know enough at the beginning to pledge yourself to your partner for a lifetime—no matter what happens?

We haven't even begun taking this problem seriously enough! I repeat, as a society we have literally shut our eyes to the enormity of the issue. We have hoped that we and those we love will somehow find the right mates. We desperately need to do better than simply shutting our eyes and hoping.

What exactly are we doing when we ask ourselves whether a particular person will be the right person for us for a lifetime?

More than anything else, we are looking into our own life and the life of another person to see what the two of us are made of. Obviously, we are attempting to follow the principles that I have outlined in this book. But fundamentally, we are trying to determine if we and this person have what it takes to say: "We *will* make it together no matter what! I *will* keep trying with you until one of us dies." It is imperative that there be this kind of dogged determination to love, honor and cherish, to perform all your duties, to faithfully care for your mate through every kind of circumstance that may come your way. It is this kind of commitment that you must be able to pledge before you allow yourself to be caught up in marriage plans.

The fact is that if we treat marriage as a "business deal" it may well be too risky. In many cases, we may not be able to gather enough data to make an air-tight decision.

The fatal flaw of our society is that the principles of business have increasingly infiltrated our intimate relationships. That's why society has found it necessary to trivialize wedding vows, to pretend they are no longer binding or relevant. Marriage makes very little sense when viewed from a business perspective. Let me explain:

Two fundamental principles in business are: (1) What you pay for something is based on what you get in return; (2) When a business arrangement is no longer a "good deal," you either alter the arrangement or terminate it.

But marriage is radically different! It depends on *unconditional* commitment. When you get married, you pledge to love, honor and cherish another person for a lifetime. If your mate changes over time, you are not released from your pledge.

When the "deal" of marriage doesn't go the way you want, you don't terminate it. You keep on loving and honoring. When your partner gets terribly ill, maybe even terminally, you keep on cherishing. If the excitement of your relationship vanishes, you keep on. If your partner falls prey to an addiction or gets depressed or loses faith in God or treats you unfairly, you don't end your relationship.

After years of working with couples struggling to stay together, I have concluded that marriage is almost never a good "business deal." It is folly to think that you can ever know enough about another person to be assured that marriage will be a good deal for the next 40, 50 or 60 years. What is a good deal now may sour a few months or years down the road. If you continually examine how beneficial and rewarding the relationship is for you, you'll be disappointed time after time.

Besides, if you regularly evaluate how well your marriage is "paying off," your relationship will suffer horribly. Relationships that are conditional allow almost no room for trust and intimacy. They become superficial and stale. It is *unconditional* love that makes marriages soar above the sordidness of our society. You must love your mate simply because you pledged to, even when the "deal" is temporarily or permanently less favorable than it once was.

## Some Awful Questions About Commitment

As I write this chapter, I find myself wondering if you think I am out of touch with the real world. Perhaps you know marriages that are so troubled you can't imagine I would suggest they should continue. Maybe you came from a seriously troubled home in which your parents stayed together but fought and argued all the time. Or perhaps you experienced the heartbreak of a marriage that came apart, and you wonder if I can understand how impossible it was for you to stick with it.

I am fully aware of how troubled marriages can become, and I know how horribly destructive a sick marriage can be for the persons involved. I have agonized with hundreds of people over their disastrous marriages. I have struggled to keep husbands and wives from killing those marriages, but I've been haunted at the same time by all the pain and anguish the family members were experiencing.

In this struggle over what to do with a problem marriage, three fundamental questions emerge:

**1.** If you committed yourself when you were young and uninformed, and now your marriage has turned out to be terribly disappointing for you, should you have to live with that commitment for the rest of your life?

**2.** Should you have to remain true to your wedding vows if your mate has a problem with drugs or alcohol, has an affair, has an explosive temper or has total disregard for you?

**3.** However strong your willpower, can it *over*power, outwit, or outwait all the problems that might occur? And if not, should you have to endure forever the awful consequences of your bad decision from an earlier point in your life?

It is not within the scope of this book to answer these questions at length. They deserve long and careful consideration. But I do want to make four general responses:

**1.** I am focusing so strongly on lifelong commitment because I believe it changes the whole way people go about building their relationship from the very beginning. If they assume their marriage will last as long as they live, they will have a totally different attitude than if they expect to walk away if things don't work out.

**2.** Far too many marriages break up that simply don't have to. Sometimes it's because the man and woman aren't willing to work as hard as they need to. They're not ready to tough it out. Other times, the partners simply don't understand what they've promised each other. They are unaware of the meaning of unconditional love. Their marriage is in trouble because they don't know what it requires.

Most of the time, I find a failing marriage is a *symptom* of problems that have little to do with the marriage itself. These marriages fail because one or both partners have not done the hard work of making themselves healthy. They blame their marriage for their lack of happiness, and when they leave their spouse for someone else, they find that same unhappiness all over again.

**3.** When marriages become sick, they need professional help. Sometimes the two people are so poisonous and destructive to each other that they have to be separated until they can do the therapeutic work to get healthy. But this in no way cancels the commitment they have made to each other. In fact, emotional, physical or spiritual sickness gives unconditional love the best chance to show its true character.

**4.** My most powerful concerns about ending a marriage have to do with the disastrous consequences for children. More and more studies are concluding that the children of divorce pay an enormous price. This is grossly unfair! A major reason for commitment is to protect the physical and emotional environment for children. I am overwhelmed by society's cavalier attitude about mate selection, especially when marital failure results in innocent children being hurt so deeply.

# What Are the Benefits of Commitment?

I talked to a couple the other day who have been married for 42 years. They were reminiscing about their life together, and it was clear there had been both happiness and struggle. They are two strong people who have worked hard at learning to love each other.

As they talked, I thought about the role of commitment in their marriage. I asked them if they had ever questioned their commitment to one another during the hard times. They both agreed it was their commitment to each other that had held them together during two particularly difficult times. The first time was shortly after they were married. He went off to fight in Korea, and she taught school. He almost never wrote, and because their relationship was so new, she began to wonder whether they had what it took to last. They both had all kinds of opportunities to get involved with "substitutes." But they didn't. They had made a promise to each other, and they kept it.

The second time of testing happened long after the first. After retirement, this man had begun to spend a lot of time around the house, and the two of them became a nuisance to each other. Her life was far more active than his, and she resented his slowing down. On the other hand, he had worked all his life to be free, and now he was. Her constant "goading" to get involved in this or that was offensive to him. It seemed to him that she was insensitive to how hard he had worked so he *could* rest and relax.

But there was a smile on both of their faces when he said in a soft, sure voice, "The intensity of our struggle was no match for the maturity of our commitment to one another."

Throughout this discussion, and scores of others I have enjoyed with devoted couples, I have developed a list of advantages that commitment provides for every relationship.

**1.** Commitment holds a couple together during three difficult periods in their relationship:

- *During the first two or three years.* Some studies indicate that *half* of all divorces take place in the first two years of marriage. I am not surprised, because so many people seem to discover the importance of careful mate selection during the two years *after* they are married. But if their vows were made with seriousness, they will easily weather these early storms. They will give their relationship a chance to develop, and the fragility of their relationship during these early stages will become but a memory.

• *During the flat places.* Every relationship I know has some periods when growth seems to stop, when nothing exciting happens, when boredom sets in. Pledges of lifelong loving become guidance systems of infinite value during these times.

• *During the relational "snags."* Most relationships go through times of trouble. He has career uncertainties. She is consumed by the demands of motherhood. Ill health may strike. Concerns about parents are often pressing. Money is frequently a problem. Commitment to love and cherish can save a marriage during these stressful periods.

**2.** Commitment significantly eases the fear of abandonment. It is this fear that is central to so many persons. It is often the most potent fear of all.

When we were young and unable to take care of ourselves, we worried about becoming lost in a crowd, forgotten while waiting to be picked up at school, or left alone by dying parents. Fears like these persist throughout our lives. We shudder at the very thought of abandonment.

That's why a spouse's promise to remain devoted means so much. Your partner will be loyal through every kind of circumstance. That frees you in a radical way. It allows you to be yourself at the deepest of levels, to risk and grow, to be absolutely authentic without any fear of being abandoned.

**3.** Commitment makes trust and intimacy possible. How can I share my innermost self with another person if I sense that I am being evaluated, that I may be disposed of? There is no way! But if I *know* in the deepest parts of my person that my partner is absolutely committed to me forever, what a powerful difference that makes.

When all of this is true, I can reveal things about myself that I have never revealed before. My secrets are safe. I'm joined with someone dedicated to my growth and development. Suddenly or slowly, all of my most carefully guarded feelings, memories and experiences begin to be shared. In this process, the inevitable interweaving takes place; this other person and I become one. We are woven together because we are able to trust so deeply.

**4.** On the basis of commitment, you can soar together on the wings of unnegotiated love. *This* is the kind of love that can provide "lift" to your relationship. When someone whose character you deeply respect makes marriage vows you're sure will be kept, what an absolutely bird-like experience you can have together. You are secure enough to fly together even during periods of struggle. You are not held together by relational successes but by a "blood covenant." And that kind of covenant makes for deep inner security.

A few months ago, a whale swam into a narrow harbor in a desperate and dangerous attempt to rescue its captured mate. Reading about this incident reinforced for me the universal appeal of "marital commitment," even among animals. Herring gulls, for instance, mate for life and can recognize their "loved one" among scores of gulls flying at great distances. Geese, wolves, beavers, tigers and foxes all form permanent paired relations. There is something about commitment that lies at the center of the created order. It provides a stable and enduring structure for the living of our days.

Humans could take a lesson from those in the animal kingdom who are joined to one partner for life. When we discover this kind of commitment for and from our partner, we will be on our way to the most meaningful of all human experiences.

# TEN
# Celebrate Your Marriage With the Full Support of Family and Friends

Visualize this scene: A woman is dressed in a long, flowing wedding gown, and a man in a black tuxedo stands close beside her. She has her arm locked in his. The two of them take turns exchanging wedding vows, repeating to each other all the appropriate words.

Standing at the bride's side are her sister and three closest friends—all looking magnificent. And next to the groom are his older brother and the three men he trusts more than anyone else.

On the first row are the bride's mother and father and her two younger brothers. On the other side of the aisle are the groom's parents, grandparents and his dad's two aunts who have taken a deep interest in the groom since he was a little boy.

Behind these people sit 100, or 1,000, friends, neighbors, classmates and co-workers. Each person is intent on hearing every word and watching every movement of the bride and groom.

All of this is taking place in a church, synagogue, park or public meeting hall. It doesn't matter very much *where* it is held. What matters most is what is going on in the heads and hearts of the bride and groom. And that depends to a great degree on what the two of them perceive to be going on in the heads and hearts of their mothers and fathers, their sisters and brothers, their closest friends—and all the others who for one reason or another they invited to the wedding.

If the bride and groom know that all these important people are feeling deeply satisfied and pleased about this marriage, what a contribution it makes to their own sense of pleasure about what is happening.

Now imagine that we freeze this scene. Everybody stays in place with the exact facial expression they had when the scene was first frozen. And imagine that we can go from one person to the next and read their thoughts and feelings without anyone else knowing what we are doing.

What we eagerly hope is that every person is filled with a sense of excitement about this marriage. Ideally, we would like all of these people—especially the ones who know the bride and groom best—to strongly approve of this relationship, to feel enthusiastic about it, to sense that these two people are genuinely "right" for each another.

If that is indeed what we find, this marriage has a wonderful chance to be successful, to be healthy and happy for the husband and wife and all the others who will eventually become a part of their growing family.

But if one or more of these important people have genuine misgivings about the relationship, this marriage undoubtedly has a significantly reduced chance of success. When parents, friends or stepchildren are not supportive of your relationship, the risk of marital failure is greatly increased.

## The Role of Parents and Friends in Selecting a Mate

Some colleagues and I were discussing this subject just the other day. As we talked, I concluded that there are five principles to consider regarding how much parents and friends should influence mate selection:

**1.** The bottom line always remains the same: Every bride and every groom need to make their *own* decision about marriage, one they can live with for the rest of their lives. This is their once-in-a-lifetime opportunity to select the person with whom they will share their future.

They are the ones responsible for making a good choice. If things don't turn out well, they alone must make their marriage work. They can never claim that someone else usurped their right to choose. They cannot waver in their commitment on the grounds that they were not the ones who truly decided. If they are ultimately responsible for their marriage, they must be totally free to make the final choice.

**2.** The wisdom of the decision depends on the depth and accuracy of their knowledge about themselves and their potential mate.

There is so much to know about oneself and about this other person. We all need help in this awareness process. The task is more complex than we can even imagine. Moreover, we may have blind spots—things that remain invisible to us about ourselves or the person we love. That's where parents and friends become crucial to us. They know us well—better than anyone else knows us—and they can often point out things that we might overlook or otherwise minimize. Without their help, we may march boldly into dangerous territory.

**3.** For parents and friends, there is a fine line between being overly intrusive and being genuinely honest and helpful. Parents must guard against speaking out too freely and unnecessarily damaging the romantic relationship of their child. But it is crucial for them to speak up when they have observations that may turn out to be of critical importance.

Some parents lack courage. They are well aware that their child is charging into a relationship that is fraught with danger. But in the name of being "supportive parents," they remain positive—and silent! Then they often feel heavy guilt when the marriage falls apart just as they thought it would.

I encourage parents to adopt a humble attitude in relation to their child's marital decisions. The truth is that parents don't know everything. In fact, they may be biased and mistaken. But if they will realize their own inadequacies, they should share their opinions honestly and fully with their children. Any parents who approach their child lovingly with observations gathered over many years can be of great assistance. When these observations are presented in a spirit of humility, they can have a very positive influence.

**4.** Parents and close friends can sometimes be too demanding. Because they love their child or friend so much, they may have standards for a marriage partner that are nearly impossible to satisfy. I have encountered parents and friends who seemed unable to imagine *anyone* being a good marriage partner for their child or friend.

**5.** When it comes to getting married, a bride and groom need to maintain a careful balance. It is dangerous to marry someone just because he or she satisfies parents or friends. But when your "primary people" say your potential mate is "just not right for you," it is equally dangerous to proceed as though their opinion is obviously wrong just because it doesn't agree with yours.

# Why Is It So Important to Have the Strong Support of Your Family and Friends?

I never cease to be overwhelmed by the enormity of the mate-selection task. This decision will *radically* affect everything about your existence for as long as you live. Because there is so much riding on this decision, you must be as sure as possible. In fact, I've become convinced that the confidence you have in your decision is an essential part of a successful outcome. When you deeply believe your choice is a great one, you will trust your partner more and generally behave more positively.

If the people who know you best aren't sure whether your choice is wise, your confidence is sure to suffer. But if they think your decision is brilliant, your confidence level will be significantly bolstered.

Moreover, if the people closest to you strongly approve of the person you're thinking of marrying, your support community is knit together from the beginning. I've seen many marriages make it through tough times because a caring, supportive group of close friends and relatives stepped in to offer a hand.

However, if your family and friends have little confidence in your choice of a marital partner, they will make that obvious in one form or another. And this message will make you feel insecure about your choice. If these "important others" simply don't like your partner, or don't like your partner *for you*, more serious consequences may accrue. Sometimes an isolation process occurs. People don't include you at key times. They forget to let you know about informal—or even formal—social events. They have concluded that your partnership is not a good one, and they begin early to prepare for its demise. Ultimately, they make it very hard for you and your mate; they actually increase the odds that your marriage will fail.

Apart from these contributions to failure that important people can make, you have to recognize that their opinions are often more accurate than your own. I have a relative whose family strongly warned her about the riskiness of her marital choice, but she went ahead and married the man anyway. She even had three children with him. But once the children no longer distracted the two of them from the problems in their marriage, these problems began to multiply. Eventually, they divorced, and the pain was, as always, excruciating. I couldn't help remembering how passionately her parents had pleaded with her to go slowly, to reconsider her choice. If only she had seen the wisdom in their advice.

Parents and close friends vary tremendously in their ability to help with the mate-selection decision. But I've learned to take seriously the advice of all these persons. In my experience, they frequently can see things that need to be considered. And if they find themselves unable to support your decision, they at least need to be listened to carefully.

Under the best of circumstances—especially when these people are mentally and emotionally healthy—your loved ones want you to be happy as much as you do. And although I would encourage you to "fight off" any parent or friend who thinks they are *definitely* right and you are *definitely* wrong, they indeed *may* be right and you *may* be wrong. That's why you should listen intently and process at length what they have to say.

# Winning the Approval of Potential Stepchildren

Children from a previous marriage often have strong feelings about a potential mate for their mother or father. These feelings must be handled with great sensitivity. Stepchildren can play a crucial role in determining the eventual success of a new marriage. If they are negative about their parent's new husband or wife, they can be highly destructive to the marital relationship. But they can be equally constructive if they have developed a positive attitude about the new family member.

Obviously, the opinion of a stepchild who will be living at home with the family is substantially more significant than the opinion of a grown chid who is on his own. Children not living at home may harbor ill feelings, but they will not have as much opportunity to damage the new marriage since they will not have daily interaction with the parent and stepparent. Nonetheless, the feelings of all the children will be crucial to the new relationship. These concerns must be addressed and dealt with gently and lovingly.

The ideal, of course, is to introduce each child to the potential mate early in the dating process. If the children are young, they will have nearly as much to gain or lose from the relationship as each of the marriage partners, and they should be considered "junior partners" in the selection process. If at all possible, they need to get to know the new person slowly so they can develop a relationship characterized by trust and caring. Eventually, their relationship with the new partner will need to be positive and strong or the marriage will be severely jeopardized.

I have worked with scores of families who were considering a new "acquisition." The situations are usually highly complex, and professional counseling is almost always important. But there is a way in which all of this merging can be done so the eventual union is far stronger than if no children were involved.

I remember working with a woman whose husband died of a brain tumor after a long illness. She had two children in their early teens, and she was deeply concerned that any new marriage not be a problem for them. Three or four years after her husband's death, she met a lawyer at her church, and they began to date. Early on, she introduced this man to her son and daughter. The children were troubled that their mother would even think about marrying someone else. How could she violate their deceased father that way? They wanted nothing to do with this "intruder."

I began to work with the mother and her children. What I realized immediately was that the three of them still had some grief work to do. The children had never completely dealt with their sadness about their dad's death. This sadness was so heavy for all three of them that it had been denied. My office became a safe place to cry and to express feelings they had never processed together before.

In time, the mother was able to talk about her desire to be married again, her need for a love relationship. She explained to her children that a new relationship would never detract from her memory of their father. That memory would always be present for her. And she told them she thought they needed two parents. The children struggled with her, but eventually her ideas proved persuasive.

Thereafter, she could introduce the lawyer to her children with greater hope that the three of them could develop a healthy relationship with one another. And that's exactly what happened. Although there were problems to overcome and things weren't always smooth, in time they all developed happy, fulfilling relationships.

The bottom line is this: Stepchildren are people, and all people must emotionally move beyond one relationship before they are ready for another.

Their feelings are complex and tender, and they need to be treated with dignity and seriousness. Whether there has been a death or a divorce, there is almost always grief work to do before a new marriage can be accepted and enjoyed by the children.

One thing is for sure: Having the full and free support of your children is of great value when you are contemplating a new marriage. This support is a goal worth working toward with patience and determination. When it has been reached, the payoff will contribute substantially to a happy marriage. If the goal is never reached, one must proceed with caution and concern.

My experience has taught me that when children work through their leftover feelings about a prior relationship, and genuinely experience the grief process, they are much more open to seeing the healthy aspects of a new relationship. If the new relationship is indeed a healthy one, they will usually join the bandwagon. But if they don't think it's healthy, professional family counseling is a must before any marriage should occur. Too much is at stake. Marriage is extremely challenging when no children are involved. When children are negative and uncooperative, successful marriage can become nearly impossible.

## *What Do You Do If the Opinion of Your Parents or Friends Differs From Your Own?*

If you are absolutely positive that you have found *the* person for you, but your parents or friends absolutely disagree, I suggest the following steps:

**1.** Remain as open and receptive as you can. Remember, *you* have the final decision.

**2.** Take your time! At this point, it is crucial not to hurry.

**3.** Find the right time to sit down with the objecting friends or parents and hear them out. Encourage them to tell you everything they can think of that has entered into their conclusion. Gather all the data as accurately as you can.

**4.** Carefully compare their observations with your own. Try to be as objective as you can. Are they right about this point or that one? And if so, does this change your bottom-line decision?

**5.** If there are major differences between their analysis and your own, and if you are left unsure or confused, seek some help from other friends or relatives—especially those who can help you better understand your parent or friend who is concerned about you.

**6.** Don't be afraid to seek professional counseling. A few sessions of therapy may save you from a destructive decision—or help you move ahead with more confidence.

# Parents and Friends Can Be Very Wrong

I'm certainly not trying to say that parents and close friends have any claim to superior matchmaking.

In fact, a lady sat in my office the other day and told me a story about her parents' involvement in her choice of a mate. She has been married for 28 years now—very happily—but her parents tried desperately to stop her marriage. They *knew* her choice was poor, and they "tried to tell her." They were very bright and thoughtful people, but they were terribly wrong, and if this woman had listened to them, she would have made an awful mistake.

Her parents eventually recognized that they were *systematically* wrong about all their children's choices of mates. This woman shared with me a conversation her father had with a close friend of his who was asking for advice.

"I want to tell you about my own children and their mates," her father said to his friend. "My wife and I were very much against one of our daughters marrying her husband, and their marriage has turned out beautifully. He is our favorite in-law. We were also opposed to our son marrying his wife, because she had a different religious background, but now we think she is great. We strongly supported our other two children in their choices, and both of them have been divorced for some time."

## *Sometimes Parents Are Right—and Sometimes They're Not*

I received a call one day from Jennifer Robinson. "I really need help," she said, "and I need to see you just as soon as possible. I'm in an emotional knot about my upcoming wedding. It's scheduled for August—only three months away—but my father is totally opposed to my marrying Tom, and I alternate between being mad at Dad and thinking he just might know more about all this than I do." I was able to see her that very day, and when I did, she couldn't talk fast enough.

"My dad has never thought *any* man was good enough for me," she said. "I can't imagine the man who would be enough for him. His standards and expectations are absurd. He doesn't want me to marry a human being!" Jennifer sat on the edge of her chair as she said this. She was almost too energized to carry on a conversation.

"Ever since I told my folks last summer that Tom had asked me to marry him, Dad has become more and more distant," Jennifer continued. "He has managed to be gone, or busy in his study, when Tom comes around. It was obvious that something was wrong, but I hadn't wanted to bring it up. I am tired of him making all of my decisions for me. I love him . . . a lot . . . but I would like to decide this one by myself!"

I listened to Jennifer for almost the entire first hour. I hardly said a word as she raced back and forth across her life, talking about her parents, growing up years, and her attempts to become an adult. What I came to see was how much she loved her dad—and how deeply he loved her. So much of her life had been an effort to please him, and she had pleased him greatly. But she could find *no way* to please him when it came to getting married. The fact was that

152

her dad wanted to keep his relationship with her the way it had been for 29 years. He was having a difficult time letting her go.

When we met again, I asked Jennifer to tell me about Tom and why she wanted to marry him. She obviously enjoyed telling me about him, and she was unusually capable of analyzing why he would be an excellent choice. They had all kinds of things in common—a strong faith in God, a desire to have a family, a love for sports. They were equally intelligent, similarly ambitious, and they found easy agreement on a whole series of issues. Both of them were very attracted to each other physically, they had excellent communication, and they were able to work through conflict effectively.

I found myself well on the way to being convinced, but I was trying to take my time and be objective. "What is it about Tom that your dad doesn't like?" I asked her.

"Well," she said, "Dad seems to focus on three things. He doesn't think Tom comes from an emotionally healthy family. He thinks it will be a long time before Tom can afford to provide for me in the way I'm accustomed to. And he thinks Tom is short on self-confidence."

"Are these observations accurate?" I asked her.

"There's a grain of truth in all three of them," she said. "Tom's dad and mom divorced when he was nine, and his life was hard. His mother worked—sometimes two jobs—and Tom's grandparents took care of him a lot. But they were wonderful! No one could have given him more love than they did. And he has grown up knowing his dad fairly well, because they're together every summer and every other weekend. All of this created a strong desire in Tom to build a family that won't come apart at the seams. He stresses commitment a lot, and he says that for him divorce is out of the question.

"It's true that it will be a long time before Tom can earn an income like Dad does," she continued. "I've thought about that, and it's not too important to me. Tom will be successful! He's a strong, good man, and he has a good education. He's just not as driven as Dad.

"And he isn't real articulate like Dad. He's 25 years younger! But he knows what his strengths are, and he wants to work on his weaknesses."

The more I listened, the more I suspected that Dad was the one who needed to be in my office. I asked Jennifer if she thought her dad would be willing to come and see me, and she thought he would. Later that afternoon, he called. He wasn't dominating or demanding the way I thought he might be. He simply said he would like an appointment, that he would like it soon. I saw him the next day.

We weren't very far into the hour when Mr. Robinson's eyes became damp, and he began to tell me about his most recent discussions with Jennifer. "She called me at the office yesterday and asked if we could have lunch," he said. "I told her that I had a meeting . . . and there was a long pause. I could tell that she really needed to see me, so I told her I would move my meeting around. At lunch, she told me all about her sessions with you—the things she told you about her relationship with me. We stayed at lunch for three hours!

"I listened for a long time—in a way I have never listened to her before," he continued. "I was amazed at how carefully she had thought through all the issues. I argued with her some, but it began to dawn on me that Tom is not the issue at all. The issue is my relationship with Jennifer."

I met with Jennifer's dad four times in the next 10 days. He told me about how close he had always been to her, how people had said that she looked like his side of the family, how he and Jennifer had always had similar ways of seeing things. He told me that he and Jennifer had always been more alike than he and his wife had been. He had known for a long time that he was going to have to work harder with his wife if he was ever going to let go of his "little girl."

During the next few weeks, he got involved in therapy, tried to understand himself, worked hard and brought his wife a few times. Then came the wedding. He turned that wedding into a celebration of Jennifer's marriage to Tom—and a whole lot more. It was a celebration of his own growth, his own "emancipation" of his daughter, his newfound appreciation for his wife, and his deep recognition that his relationship with his daughter wasn't ending but growing and changing.

When I saw Jennifer about a month after the wedding, she introduced me to Tom. They spent an hour telling me how things had gone. "My dad," she said, "couldn't have been more supportive. He told me how much he loves me, how much he admires me and how committed he is to our marriage. And he told me some of what he has found out about himself."

This was one of those times when I was deeply grateful for the process of psychotherapy. However primitive it is to "talk through" our issues, the fact was that Tom and Jennifer had celebrated their marriage with the *full* support of their family and friends. That never could have happened if Jennifer and her parents had not had the courage and the determination to seek some professional assistance in the discovery of their true selves.

What I have to tell you, though, is that for every story about a parent who was wrong in their objections, there are plenty of stories in which they were right. I have worked with hundreds of marriages that were in big trouble, and parents had often predicted the trouble well before the beginning of the marriage. They certainly are not experts in any technical sense, but when your parents or close friends see trouble, be very cautious! They are right often enough that you cannot disregard their opinions. It's certainly not a happy task to face up to their concerns. It's so much easier to pretend that they don't know what they're talking about, that if you just ignore them, they will eventually climb on your bandwagon.

Sometimes you just can't get away from the fact that parents or friends see little wisdom in your decision. When this happens, the crucial thing is to make every effort to treat each person's feelings with great care. The search is for "the truth"—the best possible decision in light of *all* the data—and if everyone will cooperate, that search will usually turn out well.

But I advise you to make every possible effort to bring each person on board. Through all of this, I suggest that you reflect on the situation as deeply as you know how, pray passionately for wisdom, follow the principles in this book, and focus intently on your mate and the promises you are making to each other.

# What If Parents and Friends Are Certain About Your Choice But You're Not?

Don't go forward with the wedding!

It doesn't matter very much what your parents and friends think if *you* are not convinced. It's *you* who is getting married, and you are the one who needs to be confident about your decision.

Sometimes I think parents become focused on the wedding itself—how they're going to appear to their friends and business acquaintances. They don't want you messing up their "biggest of all parties" by questioning whether this is the right person for you to marry. If the church has been booked, the flowers ordered, the nonrefundable deposits made—and *especially* if the invitations have been sent out—it's easy for parents to become more and more *positive* that this is the *perfect* person for you to marry.

Take it from me—or from your own common sense! This is dangerous reasoning, and though I understand the inner trauma a parent experiences around a major social event like this, the fact is that if *you* are not positive that this is the right person for you, the wedding should be delayed or canceled.

I have heard people reason that "everyone gets cold feet as the day grows near." But disregarding "cold feet" about something as crucial as this is like doing nothing about chest pain accompanied by tingling down your left arm. It's simply too important to take casually.

## "We Think You and Jon Are Wonderful for Each Other!"

As I write this, our youngest daughter, Lindsay, is preparing to be married in only 29 hours. Since the wedding will take place in our backyard, our home is alive with activity. Family and friends are arriving from all over; people will be present from 14 states and one or two foreign countries.

Lindsay and Jon have gone together for over four years, and their love and trust have grown to the point that both their families are enthusiastic about their future. Because Lindsay's dad was so involved in mate-selection theory, imagine how high the standard has been for these two. They may have wondered why they had to have someone close to them who just happened to be writing a book on the subject.

But our whole family is excited about this partnership, and I can imagine that our enthusiasm is part of the reason that Lindsay seems so deeply happy. We could hardly contain ourselves when Jon arrived this week from Russia, where he is involved in an import-export business. And his whole family will be here from Denver and many other cities to demonstrate their support for the marriage. Most of the 41 rooms we reserved in a local hotel will be filled with Jon's family and friends who are eager to say "we approve, and we're behind you 100 percent!"

When Jon and Lindsay leave for Russia in a week or two, they will take some indelible memories with them. They will remember four rapid-fire days when celebrations of their love for each other were occurring at family parties, showers and prenuptial dinners. They will never forget the cheers and the toasts, the hugs and the kisses, the countless ways their parents and grandparents, their brothers and sisters, their friends of all ages, even their niece and nephews, tried to tell them of their love and best wishes. They will hold within their hearts a clear memory of the approval and support we all feel for the partnership they are establishing and the family they are launching.

What all of us are trying to say—from Jon and Lindsay's two grand-mothers to their little niece and nephews, Marylyn, Matt, Max and Joey—is that we want them to have an uncommonly happy marriage. We are ready to do everything in our power to help them! The fact is that our loud "Yes" to them means that we are ready to become partners in their quest to build a life together that will last forever and bring joy and peace to every person who encounters it.

In days like these, couples need all the support they can get from the people who know them best. Great marriages require great support systems. If this support is absent, it needs to be pursued. If it's permanently unavailable, it's a great loss. But when it exists, it is a prize of tremendous value. It's well worth celebrating! That's exactly what we plan to do tomorrow afternoon.

# Conclusion

After analyzing the most recent sources of data about the health of families in the United States, Professor Norval D. Glenn of the University of Texas concluded in his 1992 *American Demographics* article: "If current divorce rates continue, about two out of three marriages that begin this year will not survive as long as both spouses live."[1]

The massive breakdown of the American family is threatening to overwhelm our society. In addition to the horrendous heartache suffered by all these husbands and wives, most children in our country are spending a substantial part of their childhood living away from one of their parents. This clearly sets in motion an unending series of generational waves of divorce and emotional fragmentation.

When will our collective suffering end? Not until our society recognizes one indisputable fact: People don't know how to select marriage partners in our country! We have created emotional chaos at the base of the American family because we have not faced reality. People cannot choose a marriage partner wisely without help. Romantic feelings lead us down blind alleys! Basing the choice of a mate on a set of passionate urges is insane. It leads inevitably to disappointment and failure. Ultimately, the viability of our society's corporate life is threatened.

# *Is There Hope?*

Yes! The selection of a person to marry can be accomplished with a substantial amount of wisdom. Single persons in our society can be taught how to choose a mate with whom they can be happy for a lifetime. One research study after another strengthens our confidence that wise mate selection greatly increases the chances of a happy and enduring marriage.

A few years ago I read the results of a thesis completed by Blaine Flowers for his master of arts degree at the University of Minnesota. The study was entitled "PREPARE As a Prediction of Marital Satisfaction." Flowers surveyed 148 couples who had taken a premarital test called PREPARE an average of two years prior to the study. Of the couples surveyed, 59 were now "very happily married," 53 were "unhappily married (divorced/separated)" and 36 had canceled their marriage plans after taking the test.

Flowers compared the premarital scores of these couples. Surprisingly, he found that on the basis of their PREPARE scores he could predict with 86 percent accuracy which couples would eventually be dissatisfied and with 79 percent accuracy which couples would be satisfied. According to his results, the couples who canceled their marriage plans were wise because their test scores were similar to those of the dissatisfied couples.

Studies like this one give us hope! There obviously is order in all this mate-selection chaos. We no longer need to stand by while people get married who never should. We do not have to pretend that we simply don't know what makes for great marriages or marital failures. We can initiate a strong national program to educate and counsel single persons about the wisdom of their selections. As simple as this sounds, such a program would be revolutionary in this society. And it is literally a revolution we need in America. Whatever contribution the faulty selection of mates has made to the breakdown of American families, that contribution can be reduced dramatically.

# *The Principles Are Crystal Clear*

We do not have to act like blind persons searching in the dark. The signs of good marriages and failure-prone marriages are well established. Consider in rapid summary our straightforward principles:

### *Principle #1: Eliminate the seven deadly mate-selection errors.*
**1.** Don't get married too quickly. Longer courtships produce consistently healthier marriages.
**2.** Don't get married too young. Wait to get married until you know yourself well, and until you know well the kind of person with whom you can be happy. This usually means that first marriages will not begin until the mid to late 20s.
**3.** Don't be too eager to get married, and don't let anyone else who is overly eager push you into marriage. Make sure your mind is clear and settled.
**4.** Don't try to please someone else with your choice. You are the one who will profit from or suffer from your choice for a lifetime.
**5.** Don't marry someone until you know him or her in a lot of different ways. You can make a far more accurate prediction about how much you will enjoy being married to a person if your experience base is broad.
**6.** Don't get married with unrealistic expectations. Marriage isn't a panacea; it requires an incredible amount of hard work. Don't allow yourself to expect too much from your marriage.
**7.** Don't marry anyone who has a personality or behavioral problem that you're not willing to live with forever. These problems don't vanish; in fact, they often get worse. "Miracle cures" are far easier to come by before you

are married. If the problem *can* be cured, make sure it is cured *before* you are married.

***Principle #2: Develop a high degree of conscious clarity about the person you wish to marry, and filter this image through your conscious mind until you are completely comfortable with it.***

***Principle #3: Make sure the person you marry is very similar to you.***

***Principle #4: Get married only if both you and the person you want to marry are emotionally healthy.***

***Principle #5: Make sure you are passionately attracted to the person you want to marry, but wait until you are married to express the full intensity of your passion.***

***Principle #6: Decide to get married only after you have experienced a deeper, more stable kind of love. Passion may fade, but this kind of deeper love endures.***

***Principle #7: Develop mastery in the area of verbal intimacy. The love of two people who know how to be intimate with each other will grow dramatically.***

***Principle #8: Learn how to resolve differences before you get married. This will keep the road to love free and clear.***

***Principle #9: Get married only when you are ready to be absolutely committed to your partner—no matter what—for a lifetime.***

*Principle #10: If your parents, relatives and close friends support your contemplated marriage, celebrate with them! If they don't, listen carefully to them before you make your final decision.*

# These Principles Are Demanding

I am keenly aware that following all of these principles may be extremely difficult. Nevertheless, a careful observance of each of them will significantly increase your odds of a lasting and satisfying marriage. To ignore any one of them is to take a substantial risk of ending up in the enormous group of people whose marriages break apart.

There is no need for that to happen. You and the right person can form a loving relationship that will provide an endless source of satisfying experiences for as long as you live. And if you do, no amount of preparatory work will have been too demanding.

# Love in an Enduring Relationship Is the Finest Prize

I am convinced that this life offers nothing comparable to the love of a man for his woman, and a woman for her man. When you find that soulmate for whom you have longingly searched, you will be at the beginning of a relational journey filled with joy.

In the middle of a world that is so conditional—so stern and begrudging—the discovery of a lifetime partnership with a lover is the closest thing possible to heaven on earth. To be loved forever by the person you most love is a God-given experience. I hope very much that you will have it. It is in your pursuit of this kind of ecstasy—deep love within marriage—that I trust this book will be of value.

# Notes

## Introduction

1. Margaret Kent, *How to Marry the Man of Your Choice* (New York, N.Y.: Warner Books, 1987).
2. Sylvia Ann Hewlett, *When the Bough Breaks* (New York, N.Y.: Basic Books, 1991).
3. Jessica Gress-Wright, "Liberals, Conservatives and the Family," *Commentary*, April 1992, 43-46.

## Chapter 1

1. Kelly Grover et al, "Mate Selection Processes and Marital Satisfaction," *Family Relations*, vol. 34, 1985, 383-386.
2. Tom Lasswell and Marcia Lasswell, *Marriage and the Family* (Belmont, Calif.: Wadsworth Publishing Co., 1987), 167.
3. John Welwood, "Intimate Relationship As Path," *The Journal of Transpersonal Psychology*, vol. 22, no. 1, 1990, 54-55.

## Chapter 2

1. Harville Hendrix, *Getting the Love You Want* (New York, N.Y.: Henry Holt & Co., 1988), 36.
2. Ibid., 44.
3. Lasswell and Lasswell, *Marriage and the Family*, 56.
4. Stanley Woll, "So Many to Choose From: Decision Strategies in Videodating" *Journal of Social and Personal Relationships*, vol. 3, 1986, 43-52.
5. Nick Stinnett, "Strong Families: A Portrait," *Toward Family Wellness*, edited by D. Mace (Beverly Hills, Calif.: Sage Publications).

## Chapter 3

1. J. Phillippe Rushton, "Genetic Similarity, Human Altruism and Group Selection," *Behavorial and Brain Sciences*, vol. 12, 1989, 503-509.

2. Stephen White and Chris Hatcher, "Couple Complementarity and Similarity: A Review of the Literature," *The American Journal of Family Therapy*, vol. 12, no. 1, 1984, 15-25.

## Chapter 4

1. *Make Anger Your Ally* is available in bookstores or from Focus on the Family Publishing. For more information, write or call Focus on the Family, Colorado Springs, CO 80995. (719) 531-3400.
2. Harville Hendrix, *Getting the Love You Want*, 18.

## Chapter 5

1. Judith Viorst, "What Is This Thing Called Love?" *Redbook*, March 1970, 166-168.
2. Ellen Berscheid and Elaine Walster, *Interpersonal Attraction*, 2nd Edition (Reading, Mass.: Addison-Wesley, 1978).

## Chapter 6

1. Bernard I. Murstein, *Paths to Marriage* (San Mateo, Calif.: Sage Publications, 1986), 110.

## Chapter 7

1. Nick Stinnett, "Strengthening Families." Paper presented at the National Symposium on Building Family Strengths, University of Nebrasks, Lincoln.

## Conclusion

1. Norval Glenn, "What Does Family Mean?" *American Demographics*, June 1992.

## *About the Author*

Neil Clark Warren holds a doctorate in psychology from the University of Chicago and is founding partner of Associated Psychological Services in Pasadena, California. He was dean of the Graduate School of Psychology at Fuller Theological Seminary for eight years. Currently, Dr. Warren is in private practice full time and maintains an active speaking schedule. His previous book, *Make Anger Your Ally*, is also available from Focus on the Family Publishing.

## *"Finding the Love of Your Life" Seminars*

For more information regarding Dr. Warren and his "Finding the Love of your Life" Seminars, you may contact him at 2 North Lake Avenue, Pasadena, California 91101. Phone: (818) 795-4812.